T0162149

COMMITMENT TO SUSTAINABILITY

Ooligan Press is committed to becoming an academic leader in sustainable publishing practices. Using both the classroom and the business, we will investigate, promote, and utilize sustainable products, technologies, and practices as they relate to the production and distribution of our books. We hope to lead and encourage the publishing community by our example. Making sustainable choices is not only vital to the future of our industry—it's vital to the future of our world.

OPENBOOK SERIES

One component of our sustainability campaign is the OpenBook Series. *50 Hikes in the Tillamook and Clatsop State Forests* is the tenth book in the series, so named to highlight our commitment to transparency on our road toward sustainable publishing. We believe that disclosing the impacts of the choices we make will not only help us avoid unintentional greenwashing, but also serve to educate those who are unfamiliar with the choices available to printers and publishers.

Efforts to produce this series as sustainably as possible focus on paper and ink sources, design strategies, efficient and safe manufacturing methods, innovative printing technologies, supporting local and regional companies, and corporate responsibility of our contractors.

All titles in the OpenBook Series will have the OpenBook logo on the front cover and a corresponding OpenBook Environmental Audit inside, which includes a calculated paper impact from the Environmental Paper Network.

OPENBOOK ENVIRONMENTAL AUDIT

50 Hikes in the Tillamook and Clatsop State Forests

Figures are calculated for a print run of 2,000 paperbacks.

	CHEMICALS	GREENHOUSE GASES	ENERGY	FIBER	WASTE
Paper† Cover paper: 10 pt Carolina C1S, 10% PCR.	3 lbs. volatile organic compounds (VOCs) per one ton of paper used.	298 lb. reduction of carbon dioxide equivalent per one ton of paper used.	2 million BTU reduction per one ton of paper used.‡	Paper produced from approximately 23 trees used per one ton of paper used.‡	90 lb. reduction in solid waste per one ton of paper used. 1,907 gallon reduction in water consumption.
Text paper: 55# Rolland Enviro Book, 100% PCR. 2,076 lbs used.	2 lb. reduction in volatile organic compounds (VOCs); 2 lb. reduction in hazardous air pollutants.	2,147 lb. reduction of carbon dioxide equivalent.	11 million BTU reduction in net energy.	4 ton reduction in virgin fiber, the equivalent of about 25 trees.‡	780 lb. reduction in solid waste. 11,645 gallon reduction in water consumption.
Printing & Binding 25 x 38" sheets printed on ZP 5 Heidelberg Press by Thomson-Shore in Dexter, Michigan.	Heidelberg is committed to ecological and sustainable practices.	Thomson-Shore uses PRISCO Crystal Clean Gel to clean their presses.	Insufficient data.		Lamination reduces damage to books, which reduces number of unread, returned copies.
Perfect bound with hot melt adhesives.					
Cover finished with lamination film provided by Transilwrap Company, Inc. 1,542 feet used.					Transilwrap Company, Inc. uses recycling programs to reduce factory waste.
Ink Color ink by Van Son Ink Corporation.	Insufficient data.	Insufficient data.	Insufficient data.	N/A	
Black ink provided by separate company.	Insufficient data.	Insufficient data.	Insufficient data.	N/A	

This OpenBook Audit—performed by Ooligan Press—stems from our commitment to transparency in our efforts to produce a line of books using the most sustainable materials and processes available to us.

Material specifications supplied by Thomson-Shore. Some paper quantities not provided; calculations are made per ton and are not final quantities.

†Environmental impact estimates made using the EPN Paper Calculator tool at http://www.papercalculator.org.

‡Compared to paper made with 100% virgin fiber.

50 HIKES IN THE
TILLAMOOK
AND CLATSOP
STATE FORESTS

50 HIKES IN THE TILLAMOOK AND CLATSOP STATE FORESTS

Sierra Club Oregon Chapter

Ooligan Press
Portland, Oregon

50 Hikes in the Tillamook and Clatsop State Forests
© 2018 Sierra Club Oregon Chapter

ISBN13: 978-1-932010-96-1

Ooligan Press
Portland State University
Post Office Box 751, Portland, Oregon 97207
503.725.9748
ooligan@ooliganpress.pdx.edu | www.ooliganpress.pdx.edu

Library of Congress Cataloging-in-Publication Data
Names: Sierra Club. Oregon Chapter, contributing body.
Title: 50 hikes in the Tillamook and Clatsop State forests.
Other titles: Fifty hikes in the Tillamook and Clatsop State forests
Description: Portland, Oregon : Ooligan Press, Portland State University,
    2018. | "Sierra Club, Oregon Chapter"—Cover. | Includes index.
Identifiers: LCCN 2017043908 | ISBN 9781932010961 (pbk.)
Subjects: LCSH: Hiking—Oregon—Tillamook State Forest—Guidebooks. |
  Hiking—Oregon—Clatsop State Forest—Guidebooks. |
  Trails—Oregon—Tillamook State Forest—Guidebooks. |
  Trails—Oregon—Clatsop State Forest—Guidebooks | Tillamook State Forest
  (Or.)—Guidebooks. | Clatsop State Forest (Or.)—Guidebooks.
Classification: LCC GV199.42.O72 T583 2018 | DDC 796.5109795/44—dc23
LC record available at *https://lccn.loc.gov/2017043908*

Cover design by Andrea McDonald
Interior design by Hope Levy
Index by Kento Ikeda

References to website URLs were accurate at the time of writing. Neither the author nor Ooligan Press is responsible for URLs that have changed or expired since the manuscript was prepared.

Printed in the United States of America

   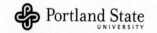

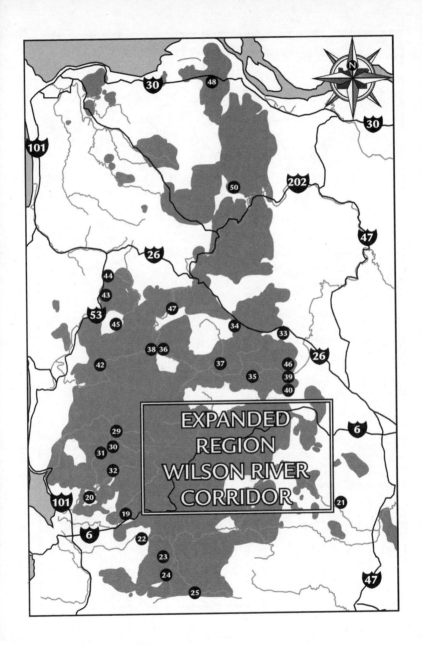

EXPANDED REGION WILSON RIVER CORRIDOR

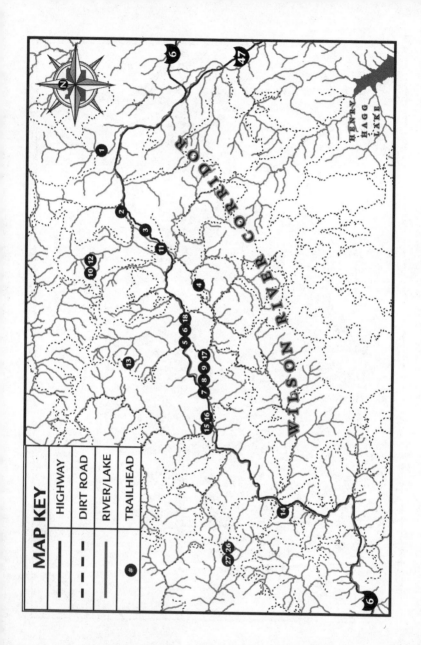

WILSON RIVER CORRIDOR

1. WILDCAT MOUNTAIN
2. GALES CREEK
3. GALES CREEK SUMMIT
4. UNIVERSITY FALLS
5. ELK CREEK
6. ELK MOUNTAIN—ELK CREEK LOOP
7. KINGS MOUNTAIN
8. ELK MOUNTAIN—KINGS MOUNTAIN TRAVERSE
9. KINGS MOUNTAIN JUNIOR
10. LARCH MOUNTAIN—BELL CAMP ROAD
11. LARCH MOUNTAIN—STOREY BURN ROAD
12. EAST STANDARD GRADE ROAD
13. WEST STANDARD GRADE ROAD TO BLUE LAKE
14. KEENIG CREEK TO FOOTBRIDGE
15. JONES CREEK DAY USE AREA TO FOOTBRIDGE
16. JONES CREEK TO DIAMOND MILL
17. KINGS MOUNTAIN TO DIAMOND MILL
18. ELK CREEK TO KINGS MOUNTAIN
19. LITTLE NORTH FORK OF THE WILSON (LOWER RIVER TRAIL)
20. TRIANGULATION POINT

TRASK-TUALATIN DRAINAGE

21. HENRY HAGG LAKE
22. THE PENINSULA TRAIL
23. GOLD PEAK
24. STEAMPOT CREEK
25. JOYCE CREEK

MIAMI-KILCHIS DRAINAGE

26. CEDAR BUTTE
27. FELDSHAW RIDGE
28. SAWTOOTH RIDGE
29. WEST END OF SAWTOOTH RIDGE
30. COMPANY CREEK
31. KILCHIS RIVER
32. LITTLE SOUTH FORK KILCHIS RIVER

SALMONBERRY-NEHALEM DRAINAGE

33. FOUR COUNTY POINT TRAIL
34. STEAM DONKEY TRAILS
35. PENNOYER CREEK AND SALMONBERRY RIVER
36. NORTH FORK OF THE SALMONBERRY TO ENRIGHT
37. NORTH FORK OF THE SALMONBERRY TO WOLF CREEK FLATS
38. LOWER SALMONBERRY TRAIL
39. STEP CREEK
40. GIVEOUT MOUNTAIN SCENIC DRIVE
41. UPPER LOST CREEK RIDGE
42. NEHALEM FALLS LOOP
43. SOAPSTONE LAKE
44. NORTH FORK NEHALEM RIVER
45. GOD'S VALLEY
46. TRIPLE C TRAIL

CLATSOP STATE FOREST

47. SPRUCE RUN CREEK TRAIL
48. GNAT CREEK TRAIL
49. BLOOM LAKE
50. NORTHRUP CREEK EQUESTRIAN LOOP TRAIL

CONTENTS

NON-LIABILITY STATEMENT

While we have made a considerable effort to check the accuracy of information in this book, errors and omissions may still occur. Changes may also happen on the land, and some descriptions that were accurate when written may be inaccurate when you read this book. One storm or logging truck, for example, can block a road, or the Oregon Department of Forestry may obliterate or change a trail.

In addition, hiking, climbing, biking, and driving in forests (especially near timber sale sites) are inherently dangerous activities. The final judgment and decision to pursue outdoor activities is always your responsibility as the user of this book. It is your responsibility to acquire the necessary skills and abilities. You must be physically fit before attempting any of the hikes described here. You must decide whether a road or trail and the weather conditions are safe for you to start or continue a trip. Road and trail conditions continually change due to timber sale activity, flooding, erosion and other natural or human-caused events. Logging and gravel trucks may meet you on forest roads. You must decide for yourself whether conditions are safe and whether you have the skills and fitness to do the hikes in this book. This book is meant only to inform and inspire.

The authors, publishers and all those associated with this publication, directly or indirectly, assume no responsibility for any accident, injury, damage or loss whatsoever that may occur to anyone using this book. The responsibility for good health and safety while hiking or driving to a hike is yours and yours alone.

FOREWORD

The names Clatsop and Tillamook apply not only to the two state forests this guide is about but to the counties the forests are in and our ancestral people, the Clatsop tribe and various bands of the larger Tillamook language group—Nehalem, Tillamook Bay, Nestucca, Neachesna (Salmon River), and Siletz (Neslets) bands of Tillamook Indians. The state forests and the lands surrounding them are their home, their gardens, their grocery, their medicine cabinet. Thousands of years of interactions between people and the land created mosaic landscapes of ancient forests, early and mid-seral forests, and open headlands, ridgetops, and meadows. Frequently applied, low-intensity fires (at proper times) maintained a prosperous and biodiverse landscape for the benefit of all.

Our Clatsop people are most known for their interactions with the Lewis and Clark party. The fort the party built and occupied in Clatsop territory over the winter of 1805–06 bore the name "Fort Clatsop." Few people, excepting a small number of Northwest Indian basketry enthusiasts, know that Clatsop basketry is some of the finest wrapped-twine basketry there is, and the work was only accomplished with materials gathered from sandy beaches and tide pools to lofty summits. Additional weaving techniques using other materials round out a rich tradition of fiber arts for our ancestors from the south bank at the mouth of the Columbia and nearby uplands north of Tillamook Head.

Not to be left out, our Tillamook basketry rivals that of their near neighbors to the north and resembles it closely. The Tillamook peoples wrought finely woven treasure baskets and tough utilitarian wares with materials from patches that their ancestors also maintained, enhanced, and gathered from.

Since the loss of lands through solemn promises not kept, these ancestral landscapes have been undeniably altered by road building and other development, harvest of the biggest and most ancient stands of timber, then the catastrophic fires of the early-mid 1900s (the Tillamook Burn), and, when the smokes cleared, the gargantuan efforts to restore an overcooked ecosystem. The objective was to plant and promote regrowth of the most merchantable timber species: Douglas-fir (Oregon's state tree). The diversity of forest species was reduced with that effort, but it is being reclaimed with today's restoration efforts. There remain many hints of the original grandness of these northwest Oregon wonders—the landscapes and the forests. With each year that passes since the Tillamook Burn era, those memories, that legacy, come back into clearer focus through the mists of time carried on coastal breezes.

As you trek, wander, or stroll through these recommended hikes, remember you are in a special place. If it suits you, think of the people who came before you—their epic struggles to maintain themselves and their place in the world, their care for these homeland landscapes, their moments of serenity in like surroundings, and their sense of wonder and thankfulness for those who came before them to make this place what it is: thoroughly Clatsop and Tillamook country. No other place quite like it.

Robert Kentta
Cultural Resources Director,
The Confederated Tribes of Siletz Indians

A MESSAGE FROM THE SIERRA CLUB

In 2017, the importance of Oregon's state-owned forests was made ever clearer by the near sale of the Elliott State Forest on the south Oregon coast. The Elliott differs slightly from the Tillamook and Clatsop forests in terms of management expectations and ecology. However, all of these public lands share the critical ecological importance of being relatively intact anchors within a sea of private, industrial timberlands along Oregon's coast. Moreover, it is *state* forests that Oregonians have the most control over; we can access them freely, weigh in on their management, and be true stakeholders in their futures.

The Elliott is not alone in facing the threat of privatization. Even before the nationwide fear of losing public lands heated up, the Tillamook and Clatsop quietly encountered this possibility. The Oregon Department of Forestry convened a stakeholder group from 2013–2014 in an attempt to gain consensus about the management of the Tillamook and Clatsop. One proposal, which was brought forth by a representative of a logging company, was the sale of these forests. The idea was never seriously considered, but there is clearly an interest in seeing these forests logged at the highest rate possible.

The near sale of the Elliott garnered national headlines and mobilized diverse public-lands activists across the state. We hope that it also helped Oregonians realize the continued importance of our state forests and remain vigilant about keeping them public *and* protected.

Chris Smith
Member, Sierra Club Oregon Chapter

INTRODUCTION

Light filters through the treetops to the dewy ferns below. Clover-shaped sorrel carpets the earth along a trail and tiny yellow wood violets dot the forest floor. Here and there, huge charred stumps decay gracefully amid living browns and greens. A creek glides by and a salmon darts through the spray in a silvery flash on its upstream journey home. It's amazing that a serene place like this—a place in the Tillamook or Clatsop State Forest—can be found within an hour of downtown Portland. Although people are discovering this beautiful landscape, it's possible to hike here and not see another person all day long.

The Tillamook State Forest provides hundreds of thousands of acres for outdoor recreation in the largest expanse of publicly owned land in northwest Oregon. Highways 6 and 26 intersect the forest, providing easy access to its wild lands. Hunters, campers, anglers, hikers, mountain bikers, horseback riders, off-highway vehicle users, canoers and kayakers, and wildlife and plant enthusiasts can all enjoy the Tillamook State Forest today.

The Tillamook State Forest encompasses the only intact watershed on the north coast of Oregon. The water quantity and quality of the forest's rivers are important to coastal communities, fisheries, and inland communities alike.

The Trask-Tualatin River system, for example, provides water to residents and businesses in Beaverton, Tualatin, Hillsboro, and Forest Grove. The forest is also home to threatened and endangered fish. Three hundred and thirty miles of waterways support runs of chinook, coho, and chum salmon, as well as steelhead and cutthroat trout. While many of these anadromous fish populations have declined sharply in the last several decades, the Tillamook State Forest still boasts some of the healthier runs of wild fall chinook in Oregon and the healthiest population of winter steelhead on the north Oregon coast. While some of these runs are healthy, others are threatened and face an uncertain future.

Illustration courtesy of Lori LaBissoniere

With its low elevation and ample rainfall (up to 200 inches per year in some places), the Tillamook State Forest also functions as a habitat anchor and refuge for many animals. Roosevelt elk, black-tailed deers, black bears, cougars, and bobcats make their home in this forest along with numerous rodents, birds, amphibians, and reptiles. More than 70 wildlife species in this forest have been identified as sensitive, threatened, or endangered under state and federal laws. Birds of special concern include peregrine falcons, northern spotted owls, marbled murrelets, bald eagles, and northern goshawks. Amphibians and reptiles that need special protection include Cope's giant salamanders, tailed frogs, and western pond turtles.

Origins of the Oregon Coast Range

What we know today as the Oregon Coast Range emerged from subduction and volcanic cataclysms about 30–50 million years ago. After that, the earth continued to erupt and metamorphose; between 8–15 million years ago enormous basalt lava flows arrived from eastern Oregon, forming peaks and headlands including Neahkahnie Mountain, Tillamook Head, and Saddle Mountain. Endless rain helped further erode and shape the Coast Range, also providing cool nourishment for the forest of Douglas-fir, Sitka spruce, western hemlock, and western redcedar that has cloaked these hills for nearly 7,000 years.

Humans have occupied the Northwest for about 10,000 years. The trade-powerful chinook Indians lived along the shores of the Columbia River, from the Pacific to the great upriver fishing sites at Celilo Falls and The Dalles. A band of chinooks, the Clatsop, called the estuarine lands around present-day Astoria and Seaside home. To the south, between what we call Tillamook Head and the Siletz River, lived bands of the Tillamook Indians: The Nehalem, Tillamook, Nestucca, and Siletz. Their Salish language sounded nothing like the chinookan dialect the Clatsop spoke, just as Salishan and chinookan myths and customs differed. But both cultures overlapped where their territories did, at Nehalem Bay and in Seaside. And a similar geography offering the same flora and fauna led to a shared way of life that stretched up and down the entire northern coast.

The Native people of this coast resembled one another in appearance. They practiced head flattening, wore tattoos and paint on their body and face, and the men boasted a dentalium septum pendant. The women dressed in buckskin leggings, shredded cedar bark skirts, and a black apron made of grass or bark; the men in loincloth or skin pants and shirts of buckskin. They had capes of beaver, fur blankets from animals like sea otter and bobcat, and hats made of reeds or cedar. The Clatsop and chinook lived all but the late summer months in permanent villages at tidewater. River mouths, estuaries, and nooks along the sea shore provided easy food—clam digging, fishing, bird gathering—and transportation by canoe. Villages consisted of several or more houses, with typically two or more families per home. Cedar planks up to three feet wide and six inches thick, hewn with elk horn, fire, stone, or even beaver teeth, covered the walls and roof. They built rectangular houses, 25 to 40 or even 100 feet long, and often dug them a few feet into the earth for added warmth. Roofing styles varied—the Clatsop favored a gabled design, while many

Tillamook homes had a single slanted roof. In winter, they told stories and performed spirit dances indoors. In summer, many families traveled to traditional spots for fishing, gathering, and hunting.

Outside of summer, the northern coast Natives seldom entered the deep forest, which to many of them was a tangled, dark, dangerous place where wolves and bears ranged, and where evil spirits roamed. Most travel was by canoe or along beaches, but forest trails did lead north and south, and east to the Willamette Valley.

At upstream falls, the Tillamook and Clatsop lived in portable mat houses while they caught and smoked or dried steelhead trout and chinook, coho, and chum salmon for winter. Others would venture a bit into the hills to pick fruits like salmonberries, huckleberries, and salal, or to dig for camas, a nonnative bulb obtained from inland. They dried the berries into cakes to eat with warm fish oil in winter, and they stored the cooked camas in loaves.

Like other Native groups throughout the Pacific Northwest, the Clatsop and Tillamook used fire to improve yield at gathering spots. Shoots and berries grew quickly in the burned clearings, attracting Columbian black-tailed deer and Roosevelt elk, whose dried meat added to the staple diet. Hunters preferred the pit or deadfall ambush, more accurate than bow and arrow, and accounts exist of Indians driving elk herds off cliffs at Saddle Mountain east of Seaside.

Thanks to the bounty of food from sea and land, tribes along the Northwest Coast were able to create elaborate

Illustration courtesy of Lori LaBissoniere

societies. Of all the coast Indians, the Salish and chinookan peoples were some of the region's most affluent, developed, and powerful.

All in all, the forest provided most of what the Natives needed for both survival and a comfortable, cultured life. Trees yielded instruments like bowls and spoons as well as boards for making shelter, while plants like bracken fern meant important nutrients and a desired item of trade. Forested streams gave salmon a place to spawn. But more than anything else, the western redcedar proved itself essential in the arts as well as in daily use. "Tree of Life" or "Long Life Maker," they called it. The bark provided clothing, rope, medicine, baskets for clamming, and cradle bedding. Its wood was used for houses, masks, canoes, and salmon harpoon shafts. The roots lent themselves to weaving, and the scaly leaved boughs served in the process of steaming food.

Euro-American
Contact and Settlement

Europeans began cruising the Northwest Coast during the late 16th century in search of the Northwest Passage and valuable furs. But the first recorded contact between Euro-Americans and the Tillamook didn't occur until two centuries later. In 1788, American fur trader Robert Gray entered Tillamook Bay, where he was greeted by Indians in large canoes holding 20-plus men and laden with food. The trading went well for a few days, until some of Gray's men landed ashore, and a cutlass was stolen from Gray's African slave, who died in the melee that followed.

In 1792, Gray returned in another ship, the *Columbia Rediviva*, and entered a broad estuary with a surly bar. He sailed east, the first Euro-American to navigate the river he named after his ship and claimed for the young United States. Along the lower Columbia, Gray traded peacefully with the chinook, who seemed to have already encountered white traders.

The most famous of meetings between the two civilizations came during the winter of 1805–1806. Lewis and Clark built their fort in Clatsop territory and documented much of what they observed, including the efforts of Clatsop and Tillamook making oil from a beached whale at today's Ecola State Park. Then, in 1811, Clatsop leaders helped a newly arrived crew of Americans choose a spot for their new trading outpost, called Astoria.

By 1841, a Methodist mission stood on Clatsop Plains; it closed less than two years later. But in 1851, a group of white settlers arrived in Tillamook country. "The Indians generally seemed pleased with the prospect of having the Whites settle among them (Poor Fools)," one of them wrote.[1] These men brought a new flag, a new religion and way of life, dairy cows, a craving for land and resources, and more diseases like the ones already spread by seafarers and trapper-traders. The Indians were quick to acquiesce both to the white settlers' demands and to the ills of maladies like small pox and alcoholism. By the early 1850s, some 90 percent of the lower Columbia River Indian population had succumbed to epidemics. Fewer than 200 Tillamook remained: Lewis and Clark had estimated them to number 2,200.

Treaties were drafted in 1851 ceding Tillamook and Clatsop land to the United States, but Congress refused to ratify them until the 20th century. Some of the villagers moved to the Grande Ronde Reservation—others stayed put. The last of the Tillamook tribe, all elderly women,

1   John Sauter and Bruce Johnson, *Tillamook Indians of the Oregon Coast* (Portland, OR: Binfords & Mort, 1974), 185.

lived until the 1920s in a camp called Squaw Town, on the Miami River, where they wove baskets and retold tales of the old days. The bulk of this country belonged to someone else now, right or wrong. And what a magnificently timbered land it was—for the time being.

Logging

Oregon's north coast remained scarcely settled for much of the 19th century. Inhospitable climate aside, a thuggish ocean and mountains of impossibly dense forest blocked the way in. The tricky, sometimes deadly entrances to fresh water deterred Euro-American settlement even more. The rocky Siletz River mouth, the rough bar at Tillamook Bay, and the Columbia River bar, one of the toughest on earth, intimidated all but the Natives. Captains refused to risk their schooners and tugs, which prevented development, because punching west through the thick Coast Range seemed out of the question.

Nature couldn't hold supreme forever, though, and the white settlers slipped in, past the river bars and the dwindling Native communities, to set up small canneries and mills on the bays. Joe Champion arrived first in Tillamook Bay in 1851, followed from Astoria by Henry Wilson, who brought the first dairy cows. The earliest mill near Astoria opened in 1844, some 30 miles upriver, with hopes of shipping logs overseas, but the vicious Columbia bar hampered business. By 1870, three sawmills operated in

Tillamook County, population 408, serving the locals who had come to make a living on milk, not trees. But by the end of the century a timber boom had begun on Oregon's north coast, the practically impenetrable Coast Range proving itself more impassable than the river bars. The "cargo mills," as they were called, serviced Pacific markets instead—places like San Francisco, Chile, Hawaii, Japan, China, and Australia. More and more settlers landed in and around Tillamook, and the tidewater forests turned to stumpscapes.

Men cut the ancient forest using axes until they learned it could be done easier and quicker with two-man saws. They hauled the dismembered trunks to a waterway or mill first with oxen, then, after its invention in 1881, using a "steam donkey" winch, and later with trains. Or they made "splash dams": plug up a creek, fill the resulting pond with logs, and blast the plug with explosives, so the timbers would rampage down to a bay, destroying the fragile stream bed and riparian zone in the process.

Each improvement in transport let loggers forge deeper into the

Illustration courtesy of
Lori LaBissoniere

woods up and down the coast. Meanwhile, mills switched from circular to band saws, allowing them to process bigger logs at a more profitable pace. The big timber companies, who had already removed the forests of America's East and upper Midwest, competed furiously with each other. Cutting sometimes at a loss, future Goliaths like Weyerhaeuser hustled to fell and market as much timber as possible, not in the least worried about the land post-clearcut. Cut and run, it was called, and instead of replanting, the land was left devastated.

The greatest impediment to liquidating Oregon's coastal forests proved topographical, and the solution awaited in the form of locomotives. Toward the end of the 19th century, big money, aided by political grease, moved in to lay railroad tracks across the northern Coast Range. Logging companies began operating their own narrow-gauge lines outside of towns like Seaside, but the coastal forests weren't merchantable east of the mountains until the all-important connection to Portland had been made.

Astoria, in its unsuccessful race to outcompete the docks in Portland, managed to snake a set of rails along the Columbia River by 1898. The Tillamook line, however, had rougher terrain to confront, and didn't connect with Portland until 1911. Logging camps and towns sprouted up alongside the new train lines. Trees fell and reached the big city faster than ever. Gone were the cargo mill days of exclusively Pacific Coast markets. With trains, the Clatsop and Tillamook forests could now travel east across the entire continent.

The Timberman newspaper gives an idea of how overproductive the Northwest logging industry had become by the early 20th century. An article from the paper's June 1920 edition relates a purchase by the Crown-Willamette Paper Co., of West Linn:

> A tract of 17,500 acres of timber . . . four locomotives, 30 sets of logging cars, 18 donkey engines, a machine shop and 15 miles of standard gauge railroad built through the heart of the tract in 1918. . . . [Crown-Willamette's] holdings, together with the one lately acquired, are estimated to contain 2,400,000,000 feet of timber.

For an idea of scale, the company's privately owned forests would fit on half a million logging trucks.

Throughout the early 20th century, Oregon's forests continued to suffer under axe and saw. And then, one scorching August day in 1933, civilization combined with nature's unalterable order to create another dire tragedy in the Tillamook and Clatsop woods.

The Tillamook Burn

In the forest's life cycle, the role of fire is regenerative. After a forest fire, different species of plants, trees, and animals can live in the previous forest's place—life gets renewed. Still, fires like the Siletz in 1849, and Oregon's largest, the Silverton in 1865, claimed 800,000 and

900,000 acres, respectively. Humanity may have been behind both. But by 1933, much of the state had already been cut over.

Many considered the Tillamook one of Oregon's finest remaining stands of untouched forest. Douglas-firs up to 400 years old, growing since the last fire, provided a home to herds of elk and deer and to cougars and spotted owls. The land, mostly owned by Lake States timber companies, had survived the saw thanks to its remote and rugged nature and to a depressed economy. Loggers had already arrived, yet their blades were only indirectly responsible for starting the great Tillamook Burn, a series of four fires each set six years apart. In total, the Burn covered 355,000 acres—almost half the size of the county. The 1980 eruption of Mt. St. Helens annihilated an area only half the size of the Burn.

Back in the 1930s, no law existed to forbid logging on fire-hazard days. August 14, 1933, had begun with another day of clear skies and fierce east winds that brought more heat to an already searing summer. The forests had finally dried up. Humidity in the Coast Range had plunged to 20 percent. Evergreen needles went crisp, ferns drooped, and the forest floor turned to dust.

Up in Gales Creek Canyon, just northwest of Forest Grove, the Gales Creek Logging Company was busy yarding felled logs. A fire warden runner arrived in a sweat and issued orders for them to quit for the day. "One more log," so the legend goes, and the steam donkey dragged another massive trunk across the ground and other logs in its way.

Illustration courtesy of Lori LaBissoniere

Friction grew into a spark, and flames soon caught the slash of lying tree limbs. The men scrambled to extinguish the fire, but it leaped into the crown of a nearby old-growth Douglas-fir, and the blaze was out of reach.

For 10 days the fire crawled west and southwest toward Tillamook, consuming 40,000 acres as fire crews, loggers, and local men struggled to gain control. "The fire has been feeding largely on beauty," wrote Mary L. Roberts of *The Oregon Journal.* Then, just as the east winds had calmed and the sky had even delivered a few drops of rain, the forest awoke to another baking sunny day. Billowed by a renewed east wind, the fire erupted on August 24, 1933.

In less than 24 hours, more than 200,000 acres burned to black. Smoky thunderheads rose past the stratosphere, while ash and charred needles reached ships 500 miles offshore. On beaches 30 miles from the fire, ash fell like dirty snow to a depth of two feet. In the fire, rocks melted and metal liquefied. Yet only one person died: a Civilian Conservation Corps man from Illinois.

Meanwhile on the 24th, an arsonist lit the hills around Wolf Creek, off what is now Highway 26 in Clatsop County. Some 60,000 acres would roar to a char. Firefighters were helpless, and the communities dependent on logging the woods between Tillamook and Forest Grove watched their livelihoods, hiking trails, and hunting and fishing grounds expire in the darkening grip of smoke. But that night the east wind backed off, and a cool Pacific fog blanketed the infernal forests. Cooler weather settled in, allowing the 3,000-strong fire crew to make progress, and by early September the fall rains doused what fire remained; by September 5 it was out. "One more log" had cost Oregon 375 square miles of pristine forestland and an uncountable number of wildlife. Locals looked upon the rolling landscape of scorched, limbless snags in disbelief, impotence, and horror. Nobody knew what to do with such a wasteland.

Salvage operations began soon enough. Logging companies pulled what they could from the wreckage before beetles ate through it. Those old-growth behemoths proved millable on the inside, and what else were they going to cut? The Burn, as the affected land came to be called, remained vulnerable to fire, however, and in 1939 another spark set the forest ablaze again. A salvage operation may have been responsible. Either way, nearly 200,000 acres burned, much of it in the wake of the 1933 episode, with some 28,000 acres of green woods perishing to the flames. Whatever natural regeneration that had sprouted in the last six years vanished altogether.

The salvage campaign continued, and in January 1941, volunteers initiated the Burn's reforestation with help from the Department of Forestry. On the trail from the Wilson River Highway to Cedar Butte they planted Port Orford cedars that still grow there today. Little did it matter, though—by 1942, the country had focused its attention and effort on World War II. Work in the burnt forest turned to harvesting all of the salvageable wood possible—a process that imposed its own deleterious effects.

Then, on July 9, 1945, fire struck again, very near where the 1933 conflagration had begun. Fifty miles burned in the first six days. Some 4,000 firefighters, military men, loggers, and even high school students toiled for eight weeks to save what they could before the rains finally stamped it out. No less than 180,000 acres re-burned. The people of Oregon, and especially those who lived around the Burn, had reached their limit. This land needed protection from future fires and trees to make it a forest again. Governor Earl Snell sympathized, and he soon created a committee to study solutions.

Rehabilitation and Protection

No state, or nation for that matter, had ever attempted reforestation on such a scale. Plenty who had seen the Burn had already given up on replanting such an apocalyptic landscape. But others believed in the power of collective will and strong backs, including State Forester Nelson S. Rogers. Optimism inspired creative thinking. The general election ballot of 1948 included a $12 million bond measure to finance the operation. Voters narrowly approved the plan—ironically, it failed in Clatsop and Tillamook counties—and the Forest Rehabilitation Act conceived the forest we know today. Meanwhile, the affected counties agreed to transfer title of the burned land to the state in exchange for the lion's share of future timber revenue.

On July 18, 1949, Governor Douglas McKay signed the rehabilitation program into effect at a ceremony held at Owls Camp, soon renamed Rogers Camp in honor of Nelson S. Rogers, who three weeks later passed away. America's postwar momentum and ingenuity went to work rebuilding the woods. But before trees could be planted, the area required fire breaks, roads, crews, and lookout towers. Loggers and even inmates cleared 1.5 million snags (dead standing trees) from 220 miles of ridgetops and highways, and workers constructed a 165-mile road system to allow 30-minute access to vulnerable zones. A final fire, sparked in 1951, consumed little more than 30,000 acres of already-burned land surrounding the Trask River before surrendering to the new fireproof regime: the only Tillamook fire the rains didn't have to put out.

With the upcoming reforestation safeguarded from future blazes, 325 square miles of the Burn could now be replanted. Geographers re-ran boundary lines and drew maps, while foresters assessed site-specific characteristics to determine how best to proceed in each section, helping to advance forest sciences in the process. In the early 1950s, salvage operations got in the way—more than half of the burned trees were eventually converted to useable wood—until finally the logging companies moved on.

Helicopters began dropping 36 tons of Douglas-fir seed in November 1949, covering over 100,000 acres, but hand planting proved more successful. State-run nurseries provided seedlings, and eventually some 75 million two-year-old Douglas-firs (the preferred species due to its commercial prowess) found a home in the nutrient-rich, rain-drenched soil. Setbacks came in the form of hardwoods like red alder that grew fast enough to deprive the shade-intolerant Douglas-fir of sunlight. Also, winter-famished animals like deer and beaver devoured the planted seedlings, while birds and rodents ate up the sown seed. Animals ate two out of three trees, but planting crews, volunteers, and school children covered the Burn with green over the course of two decades, and by the start of the 1960s the forest had miraculously reemerged. The forest was no longer a blackened desert—the vision of Nelson S. Rogers had come to fruition.

On July 18, 1973, exactly 24 years after the rehabilitation's commencement, Governor Tom McCall presided over a closing ceremony at Rogers Camp. The bond buying and the reforestation had officially concluded. Speaking to the crowd of state forestry personnel and men and women who had fought the fires and planted new life into the hills, McCall referred to the Burn as "a monument to man's carelessness and at the same time to his dedication. And so we meet today in trembling pride," he continued, "anxious for the safety of the trees, but buoyed by seeing what Oregon has done—and can do again if we must."[2] On that July day, having survived the succession of fires and the historical replanting, the formerly burned areas became the Tillamook and Clatsop State Forests.

Governor McCall's remarks still ring true regarding a forest and the threat of flame. But as the 1970s ushered in the 1980s, a renewed attack on the Tillamook and Clatsop forestlands would call into question the "safety of the trees" and "man's carelessness." Such profit-based cutting soon made many tremble at the sight of Oregon forestry's actions and continues to do so. The "block cut," also called the clearcut, began to raze the land into a mottled patchwork of shrubs and mud.

As the second-growth Tillamook Forest came of age, timber companies—and the local counties that rely on logging revenues—pressured the state to increase cutting. In 1997, the Oregon Department of Forestry (ODF) proposed

---

2   Fick, L. R., & Martin, G. (1992). *The Tillamook Burn: Rehabilitation and Reforestation*. Forest Grove, OR.: Oregon Dept. of Forestry, p. 252.

a rule making timber production the primary purpose of our state forests. ODF claimed that timber extraction would provide Oregonians with the greatest permanent value from their forests. Numerous fishermen, hunters, recreational users, and environmentalists came to public hearings to protest this rule.

ODF couldn't ignore the huge outcry. In the final version of the administrative rules, ODF recognized the importance of fish and wildlife habitat, watershed protection, erosion and flood control, and recreation. Still, timber was the management focus of the plan subsequently approved by the Oregon Board of Forestry, leaving about 90 percent of our state forests—including the Tillamook—vulnerable to future commercial logging.

Vision for the Future

In 1999, it became clear to the Oregon Chapter of the Sierra Club that if we were to save the Tillamook State Forest, we would have to reach out to the public with the message that the natural and recreational values of this forest were worth protecting—and if there were more visitors to the forest, more people would advocate for its protection. But most people don't know much about the Tillamook State Forest, even though they drive through it on their way from Portland to the coast.

To expose more people to the Tillamook Forest in a way that had a minimal ecological impact, the Sierra Club decided to educate people on the forest's hiking opportunities. Unfortunately, there are limited official trails in the forest. As a result, people began to share hiking routes they had found on elk paths, overgrown logging spurs, little-used forest roads and railroad tracks. This guide, originally published in 2001 and covering only the Tillamook State Forest, grew from those contributions and the subsequent efforts of numerous volunteers.

The Sierra Club has a vision for the Tillamook and Clatsop State Forests that contrasts with the one proposed by the ODF. In our ecologically sensitive vision, forest reserves are permanently set aside for the protection and restoration of imperiled species; watershed preservation and outdoor recreation are deemed critical to the quality of life and the economies of local communities; and large areas of the forest are allowed to grow into the majestic old growth that once stood there.

We want future generations to be able to stand in awe of towering trees. Hence this second edition of *50 Hikes*, which now includes the beautiful, yet heavily logged, Clatsop State Forest. If you love your local forests, use the hikes in this book to remind yourself of Oregon's innate majesty, to discover new favorite trails, and, most importantly, to find the inspiration it takes to preserve a forest ecosystem as threatened and fragile as the Clatsop and Tillamook woods.

Daniel O'Neil

IMPORTANT INFORMATION ABOUT THE TILLAMOOK AND CLATSOP STATE FORESTS HIKES

A Must-Read for Hikers New to the Forest

Welcome to the Tillamook and Clatsop State Forests. This beautiful, temperate rainforest is close to the Portland metropolitan area, yet it remains relatively undiscovered by most Northwest Oregon hikers. There are plenty of hiking opportunities on trails, four-wheel-drive roads, old logging spurs, railroad grades, and angler or elk trails along streams.

The Oregon Department of Forestry (ODF) is steadily working to improve recreational opportunities and infrastructure. However, this effort is currently underfunded and is often overshadowed by a large-scale timber extraction program. This means that trail maintenance can be inconsistent and that logging operations sometimes change, impede, or swallow up existing trails. This is the second edition of *50 Hikes,* and, just as was written in the first edition in 2001, in the future "another group will have to write a new Tillamook State Forest hike book!"

This book describes not only ODF's official hikes but also several unconventional, enjoyable hikes along some of the alternative routes mentioned above. We've included a few hikes for the more adventurous who have bushwhacking and map and compass skills. We've also included a scenic drive that is derived from what used to be a hike found in the original edition of this book. Most of the hikes follow clear routes but are not marked with trail signs or trail markers. Therefore, it is of utmost importance that you carry a current, printed map with you at all times when you drive and hike in the Tillamook and Clatsop State Forests.

Safety Tips for the Tillamook and Clatsop State Forests

Carry a Map—a Real Map—Not Just a Phone

Do not drive into the Tillamook or Clatsop State Forests without an up-to-date map. While there are some hikes that start right from OR-6 or US-26, many of the hikes start at trailheads on forest roads. There are more than a thousand miles of roads in the forest—some main roads, some dead-end roads, some marked with small signposts, many not marked at all. Even with a map, it can be easy to get confused by the huge network of roads, especially when new ones are being built or old ones being obliterated.

While this book describes how to get to a trailhead, it does not map out the driving route. We recommend you buy a Northwest Oregon Protection District Map produced by the Oregon Department of Forestry. Maps are available for purchase at local ODF district offices.

Ask for the Northwest Oregon Protection District Map at one of these offices:

Oregon Department of Forestry – Forest Grove District
801 Gales Creek Road
Forest Grove, OR 97116
503-357-2191

Oregon Department of Forestry – Tillamook District
5005 3rd Street
Tillamook, OR 97141
503-842-2545

Oregon Department of Forestry – Astoria District
92219 Highway 202
Astoria, OR 97103
503-325-5451

Online versions of the maps can be found at the following websites:
http://gisonline.odf.state.or.us/protectionmapdownload/
http://www.odf.state.or.us/gis/data/Published_Maps/pdm/
   NorthwestOregon_South_2012.pdf
Please note that URLs are subject to change.

ODF has also produced a recreation map for the Tillamook State Forest which contains many of the trails in this book. Ask about this map as well. For the digital version, see the Oregon.gov ODF Recreation Map located at:

https://data.oregon.gov/Recreation/ODF-Recreation-Map/ xcxz-zb5j.

Be Careful of Logging and Gravel Trucks

The Oregon Department of Forestry calls the Tillamook and Clatsop State Forests "working forests." In other words, logging and roadbuilding can be going on any place and any time in the forest. On weekdays, it's not unusual to meet a large logging truck or a speeding gravel truck coming around a bend on a narrow gravel road. One precaution you can take, if you're planning to drive deep into these state forests, is to hike only on the weekends. There are fewer people working in the forest on Saturday and almost none on Sunday.

If you do go into the forest on a weekday, call ODF (see contact information above) to find out if you can expect to encounter any logging or gravel-hauling operations on your planned route. If you have a CB radio, you can communicate with large-vehicle drivers on your route. Look for trees along roads in the forest marked with the channel to tune in to. Be especially careful around bends in the roads.

Also, be aware that sometimes the more remote forest roads are temporarily closed by timber operations. ODF is supposed to place a sign at the beginning of these roads to alert the driver, but this doesn't always happen. Again, calling ODF before your hike could prevent you from having to turn around at a logging operation. Be sure to report to ODF if they have not marked a road closure with a sign.

Be Aware of Other Forest Users

Chances are that on many of these hikes, you won't encounter another soul the entire day. The hikes in this book are, for the most part, in the non-motorized sections of the Tillamook and Clatsop State Forests. A few, however, are not. If you encounter a motorcycle or off-road vehicle on your route, you'll most likely hear it long before you see it and have time to get out of the way. You may also encounter horseback riders. Step off the trail on the downhill side to let the horses pass. Speak to them quietly to help keep them from spooking. Mountain bikers are supposed to give you the right of way, but it's usually easiest just to step off the trail to let them pass.

You may hear target shooters in the area, so stay away from where they're shooting. If you feel in danger, blow a whistle or yell to let them know you're there. Target shooters should not be shooting blindly into the forest, so be sure to report any dangerous behavior to the forest deputies.

Be aware of hunting season in the fall—bow hunting in September and gun hunting in October and November. To be most safe, you may not want to hike at all during the gun season. If you do hike, be sure to wear bright orange or red clothing and carry a whistle.

Be Aware of the Weather

Rain is a given in the Tillamook and Clatsop State Forests for a large part of the year. If it's raining very hard, don't drive on dirt roads that may become muddy or eroded. Don't cross coastal streams during heavy rain as they rise quickly. In both cases, you may become trapped if you don't follow these precautions.

Also, be aware that the higher elevations of the forest may have snow from late winter to mid-spring. **Don't try to drive or hike in the snow in this rugged forest.**

Carry the 12 Essentials

Even the easiest hike could require the following gear if you make a wrong turn or encounter a storm. It's smart to always carry these items:

1. Plenty of drinking water and extra food
2. Warm, water-repellant clothes
3. Whistle
4. Map and compass
5. First aid kit
6. Flashlight
7. Waterproof matches
8. Sunglasses and sunscreen (for hikes in open areas)
9. Knife
10. Emergency shelter (tarp, space blanket, etc.)
11. Cell phone instructions
12. Personal identification

Before leaving on a hike, be sure to tell someone where you're going, what vehicle you're driving, and when you plan to return so that they can alert the forest deputies in case you don't get back on time. If you get lost, stay put and stay warm.

How to Use This Book

The featured hikes are divided into five regions: the Wilson River Corridor, the Trask/Tualatin Rivers Area, the Miami/Kilchis Rivers Area, the Nehalem/Salmonberry Rivers Area, and the Clatsop State Forest. Choose your hikes based on the following criteria:

- **Easy** – These hikes generally range from 1 to 5 miles round-trip and gain less than 500 feet in elevation. They're good excursions for novices or those who want only a short hike.
- **Moderate** – These hikes are generally from 4 to 10 miles round-trip. Long moderate hikes may not have significant elevation gain, but shorter moderate hikes may gain up to 1,500 feet in elevation. These hikes require fitness and rest stops.
- **Strenuous** – These hikes require top physical condition, especially cardiovascular fitness and good knees for uphill and downhill climbing. They generally range from 5 to 12 miles. The main criterion for a strenuous hike is an elevation gain of more than 1,500 feet in a relatively short distance.

NOTE

Some hikes in this book state a *cumulative* elevation gain. This means you'll have significant elevation gain in both directions because the route varies between going uphill and downhill. What goes down on the way in must come back up on the way out! Cumulative elevation gain can actually be greater than the highest point of elevation you reach on the hike.

The following key should also help you choose hikes that are appropriate for you.

 The hike is appropriate for children.

 A forest map is needed to negotiate the roads to the trailhead.

 A high-clearance vehicle is needed to reach the trailhead. A four-wheel drive vehicle may be needed in certain weather conditions.

 The trail may be inaccessible by road or partially covered by snow in winter and spring.

Horses are allowed on this trail.

 Mountain bikes are allowed on this trail.

 There are restrooms near the trailhead.

 The trail may go near an active logging area.

 The hike includes a nearby picnic area.

Enjoy your hikes and be careful!

Illustration courtesy of Lori LaBissoniere

WILSON RIVER
CORRIDOR

WILSON RIVER OVERVIEW

The OR-6 (Wilson River Highway) corridor between Banks and Tillamook is the most accessible and used stretch of the Tillamook State Forest. Both Gales Creek and the Wilson River provide gorgeous waterways across the entire route, and many small canyons and tributaries offer opportunity for off-trail adventuring to hidden waterfalls. Of course, it is the established infrastructure that makes this area more enjoyable for a variety of visitors. Numerous trailheads, picnic areas, campgrounds, and river beaches mean that, on a sunny summer day, space and quiet can be hard to find. It is a testament to the immense recreation potential and the exponential growth of the Portland metro area that this stretch of the Coast Range is so packed.

The Wilson River Trail is a collection of stand-alone sections that allows hikers to either pursue small day hiking opportunities or get ambitious and tackle the entire 22.6 miles (one way) with either an overnight or a coordinated car shuttle. Along with a great introduction to the Tillamook State Forest, the Wilson River Trail allows hikers to access the river along the way for a cooling dip in the summer or year-round fishing. The trail also connects with more strenuous opportunities including Kings Mountain and Elk Mountain.

WILDCAT MOUNTAIN

1

Suggested
Maps
2012
Northwest
Oregon
Protection
District Map

This hike, which provides sweeping views of the Willamette Valley, sticks to gravel forest roads that are generally well maintained and easy to follow, with a few steep sections.

Difficulty	Trailhead Coordinates
Moderate	45.667983, −123.291733
Distance	Elevation
9.8 miles round-trip	1,300 feet

GETTING THERE

From Portland, drive west on US-26, then veer left on OR-6 toward Tillamook. Just past milepost 39, turn right onto Timber Road. Drive 1.8 miles to an unmarked road on the right with a yellow gate. Park on the left side of the road and take care not to block the gate.

To begin your hike, pass through the yellow gate. On the right side of the road you will see a large sign letting you know you are on Wildcat Road. In about 0.1 miles you will come to a bridge over a small creek. The main road stays obvious until you reach 1.07 miles. Here you will pass under power lines, and the road splits. Take the road to the right and cross a wooden bridge over another small creek. Ignore the road that splits off to the right shortly after the bridge and continue on the main road.

If you are doing the hike in early summer, there will be a variety of flowers blooming alongside the road, including goatsbeard, foxglove, daisies, Douglas Spirea, and salmonberry.

Around 3 miles into your hike there is a fork in the road. Take the sharp left to stay on Wildcat Road. Hopefully you've saved some energy, because here the road inclines more steeply. The road levels out again at 3.3 miles. To your left is an old road with a large berm blocking it; ignore this and stay on the main road. The next mile of the hike is a pleasant series of slight inclines and declines.

At about 4.3 miles, take a sharp left, leaving Wildcat Road for a much rougher and steeper road that has recently been cleared. You will reach the end of the road and a large clearing at 4.8 miles. Here you can climb a berm at the top of a quarry for an impressive view of the Willamette Valley and the small community of Buxton.

Photo courtesy of T. J. Carter

GALES CREEK

2

A tranquil hike along a tributary of the Tualatin River. This hike features lush second-growth forest after the original Tillamook Burn.

Difficulty	Trailhead Coordinates
Moderate to strenuous	45.64231, -123.35926
Distance	Elevation
Up to 13.6 miles round-trip	About 2,000 feet elevation gain

Suggested Maps
Wild Salmon Center and Outdoor Project Wilson River Map

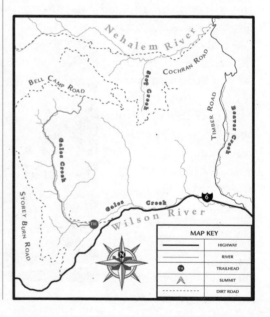

GETTING THERE

From Portland, drive west on US-26, then OR-6, toward Tillamook. At milepost 35, turn right at the sign for Gales Creek Campground and drive about a mile to the day use area. The campground is open May through October, and there is no fee for day use. Park in the lot and look for the trailhead to the left of the bridge. There should be a sign nearby that displays a map.

Follow the trail through a lushly vegetated ravine. At about 0.5 miles, look for a lone old-growth Douglas-fir (probably 200 to 300 years old) on the right side of trail. Other vegetation may include alder, red huckleberry, thimbleberry,

Photo courtesy of Riley Pittenger

vine maple, sword fern, Oregon grape, oxalises, and—in the spring—trilliums. Wildlife is abundant in the canyon—watch for birds such as chickadees and woodpeckers, small mammals such as raccoons, and elk.

At 0.75 miles, cross a wooden footbridge. After the bridge, turn right at a fork in the trail. As of this 2018 release, the trail to the left goes only a short distance, but eventually it will continue south as part of a new trail system.

From the fork, you can walk the main creek trail as far as 5.9 miles north to Bell Camp Road almost 7 miles to the north. The path continues alongside or above Gales Creek at varying distances from the stream, occasionally crossing it via wooden and log bridges. In a few places, you must step across on rocks and may get your feet wet.

As you hike, watch for small waterfalls, rapids, and log-jams. The creek even flows belowground at times. Look for trout in pools that form where the stream submerges or emerges from the ground.

Turn around when you reach Bell Camp Road at about 6.8 miles—or at any point along the way if you want a shorter hike.

Evidence of the original Tillamook Burn is still visible from the Gales Creek trail. Today, although the charred snags of the old trees are historically interesting, the main appeal of this hike is the beauty of the lush second-growth forest and the creek that runs through it. Gales Creek Canyon is testimony to the ability of this temperate rain-forest to renew itself, given the chance—and the vision of the many Oregonians who planted millions of trees in the 1950s, '60s, and '70s

The Gales Creek trail is one segment of a system of interconnected trails with Gales Creek Campground as the hub. The northern segment extends the trail for about 4 miles from Bell Camp Road to Reehers Camp on Cochran Road (with another trailhead at Cochran Bridge) in the Nehalem drainage, 2 miles west of the town of Timber. The southern segment adds another 3 miles of trail. It veers left from the Gales Creek trail at the fork and crosses Storey Burn Road (about 1 mile) to Graham Bridge west of the summit on OR-6. At the bridge, it connects with the Historic Hiking Trail to University Falls south of the highway.

Photo courtesy
of Riley Pittenger

GALES CREEK SUMMIT

A lush hiking and biking trail that follows the West Fork of Gales Creek from Wilson River Highway summit to Gales Creek Campground.

Difficulty	Trailhead Coordinates
Easy	45.64231, -123.35926
Distance	Elevation
3.4 miles round-trip	About 700 feet gain on the return

Suggested Maps ODF Tillamook State Forest Trail Guide: Gales Creek Trail; Wild Salmon Center and Outdoor Project Wilson River Map

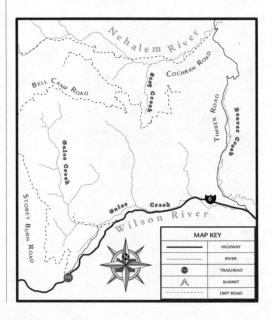

MAP KEY	
	HIGHWAY
	RIVER
TH	TRAILHEAD
⋀	SUMMIT
	DIRT ROAD

GETTING THERE

From Portland, drive west on US-26, then OR-6, toward Tillamook. Park in the parking area at the OR-6 summit at milepost 33.

Look for the trailhead on the right (north) side of the highway. Follow the well-developed trail to Gales Creek Campground 1.7 miles away. Along the way, you'll pass by steep slopes on the side of the creek opposite the trail.

This trail is near the site of a logging camp where the first of the series of Tillamook Burn fires started in 1933. Now you'll see lush second growth including Douglas-fir, alder, cottonwood, vine maple, ferns, thimbleberry bushes, and much more. Elk frequent the area, as do hawks and owls. The creek is a great place to cool off during warm weather.

Gales Creek Campground has a day use area that's a good place for a picnic. To return to the trailhead, simply retrace your steps.

Photo courtesy of Riley Pittenger

UNIVERSITY FALLS

4

This loop hike to University Falls takes you through varied woodland habitats, with the option for shorter mid-trail hikes. It offers opportunities for bird-watching, seasonal wildflowers, and waterfall views.

Difficulty
Moderate

Distance
A shorter family hike (about 2 miles round-trip) to the falls from a secondary parking area; about 4 miles round-trip to the falls and back; or 6.2 miles for the loop

Trailhead Coordinates
45.59841, -123.39234

Elevation
About 900 feet elevation gain to the falls; 2,450 feet cumulative elevation gain for the loop

Suggested Maps
ODF Tillamook State Forest Trail Guide: Historic Hiking Loop; Wild Salmon Center and Outdoor Project Wilson River Map

Photo courtesy of GiGi Peek

GETTING THERE

From Portland, drive west on US-26, then OR-6, toward Tillamook. As you approach the summit at milepost 33, watch for highway signs for Rogers Camp and the University Falls Trailhead. Just past milepost 33, turn left onto a gravel road to the left of a large open area used by ODOT as a gravel stockpile. After about 100 yards on this road, turn left onto a fire road. Drive about 200 more yards to Rogers Camp and park in the day use area parking lot. If you want to do the short 2-mile hike, do not turn left onto the road to Rogers Camp. Instead, continue on the main road to the University Falls parking area.

This trail starts in an off-highway vehicle (OHV) staging area that can be very noisy on weekends. For the most part, the trail has been designed to keep hikers and OHV users separate. However, there is a 1-mile section where the route is shared and OHVs may be encountered, especially on weekends.

The loop hike can be done in either direction. The following description starts from the trailhead at the west end of the ODOT gravel pit. From the Rogers Camp parking lot, walk back to the gravel pile and follow a trail around the back to a gate at the northwest corner. Go through the gate and walk about 0.25 miles down a gravel road. Look for the Historical Hiking Trail sign on the right. Follow this trail as it descends steeply to a bottomland with huge alders and moss-covered cedar stumps. Shortly past 0.5 miles, the trail crosses an old road. Turn left onto this road, which takes you to a new bridge over the Devil's Lake Fork of the Wilson River. Cross the bridge and bear left to follow an old road along the west bank of Elliott Creek for about a mile. This is the only part of the hike shared with OHV users; be prepared for noise and give any OHVs wide clearance.

Illustration courtesy of Lori LaBissionere

Come to a bridge over Elliott Creek; on the far side, watch for a sign for the Historical Hiking Trail, which ascends to the left. Follow the trail for about a mile to an intersection with another old road. Just before this road, note a sign for Gravelle Trail—the old name for this part of the trail. On the other side of the road is a sign for University Falls. Follow the trail for about 0.5 more miles to reach the falls, which cascade over stepped rock formations. Water volume varies with the seasons. Here you can sit on a bench or one of a series of thoughtfully placed logs and enjoy the view. Or you can find a pretty picnic area at the old road you most recently crossed.

To continue on the loop, return to the old road and follow it to the right. The road turns into a trail marked by blue dots on trees. Climb steeply for 0.5 miles until you come to University Falls Road, where there is a small parking area. This is the starting point for the short hike to the falls. Cross the road and follow the signs for the Historical Hiking Trail. The trail continues about 3 miles along some sparse copses of trees and a large clearcut before turning back into the trees to the area west of Brown's

Photo courtesy of GiGi Peek

Camp (another OHV area), then another 2 miles back to the trailhead, ending on Fire Break Road at the west end of the Rogers Camp Day Use Area.

While the trail crosses several roads and the directions may sound complicated, it is generally well-marked and easy to follow. If you have trouble picking up the trail after a road crossing, look carefully 100 feet in either direction on the other side of the road, and you should be able to find it.

The trail passes through rolling terrain and various habitats, including riparian areas, ridges, and clearcuts. In the spring, expect to see trilliums, wood violets, and other seasonal wildflowers. If you're a birder, keep ears and eyes open for wrens, juncos, bush tits, Swainson's thrushes, and kinglets. Along streams, watch for signs announcing work on riparian habitats, such as logs being placed in creeks. You'll also see large, multi-trunked alders and huge stumps charred by long-ago fires.

ELK CREEK

The trailhead at Elk Creek Campground is the starting point for hikes on the Elk Creek/Elk Mountain/Kings Mountain/Wilson River Trail system. This moderately strenuous hike along the length of the Elk Creek trail will deliver a good aerobic workout surrounded by views of beautiful Elk Creek and towering basalt cliffs. A more leisurely option follows the banks of Elk Creek along the Elk Creek and Wilson River Trails.

5

Difficulty	Trailhead Coordinates
Moderate	45.6100731, -123.4665833
Distance	Elevation
8 miles round-trip	1,800 feet elevation gain

GETTING THERE

From Portland, drive west on US-26, then OR-6, toward Tillamook. Just after milepost 28, turn right at the sign for Elk Creek Campground. Drive 0.4 miles to the end of the gravel road and park in the trailhead parking lot just across the bridge at Elk Creek. Elk Creek Campground features secluded walk-in sites with picnic tables right on the creek.

Suggested Maps
ODF Tillamook State Forest Trail Guide: Kings Mountain, Elk Mountain, and Elk Creek Trails; Wild Salmon Center and Outdoor Project Wilson River Map

Your hike begins at the north end of the parking lot where you walk up old Elk Creek Road, which the ODF has converted into a hiking trail. The path follows a clear, cold, alder-lined stream inhabited by kingfishers, river otters, and winter steelhead. In the spring, you may be able to see small fingerlings at a fish survey area near where the Wilson River Trail fords the stream.

Follow the old road grade—now a broad, nearly level trail—along the west bank of Elk Creek. In the spring, the path is lined with monkey flowers, Indian paintbrush, and lupine. After 0.6 miles, you'll come to the confluence of Elk Creek and the West Fork of Elk Creek, where the Wilson River Trail fords the main branch of the stream. Stay straight at the junction and begin following the West Fork.

At 0.9 miles, the trail begins to climb, affording views down into the log-choked streambed. Closer at hand, watch for moss-covered rock outcroppings covered with hanging fern gardens. As you continue upward, forested mountainsides and basalt cliffs—reminiscent of those in the Columbia Gorge—come into view. The trail rises at a moderately steep grade, ascending out of the canyon bottom to the slopes far above.

At 2.9 miles, the trail begins a near-level traverse of the ridge at the head of the West Fork Elk Creek canyon. Breaks in the trees allow glimpses down into the lush drainage and out onto forested canyon walls as well as more airy views of the striking basalt bluffs.

After a nearly level walk of 0.5 miles, the trail begins climbing again, finally reaching the Elk Mountain trail

Photo courtesy of
Josh Kulla

junction at 4 miles. At this point you've climbed 1,800 feet since the Wilson River Trail junction. This is a good place to turn around and retrace your steps, unless your goal is either Elk Mountain or Kings Mountain—2.8 miles and 2.2 miles distant, respectively.

If you're not up for an aerobic workout but still want to wander along Elk Creek, you should try this 1.86-miles roundtrip ramble with minimal elevation gain:

Follow the Elk Creek trail for 0.6 miles to the Wilson River Trail junction. Turn right and follow the steep path down to a bridgeless stream crossing. During low water, you'll be able to cross over on rocks to the far bank, but wading will be necessary during other times of the year.

Once across, follow the Wilson River Trail gently uphill, enjoying views of babbling Elk Creek along the way. On a clear day, sunlight shines through the alder leaves and slivers of light play on a fairyland of mosses and ferns. Watch for signs of elk and deer as you go.

At 0.33 miles from the stream crossing, you'll reach the first switchback, a good turnaround point.

6

ELK MOUNTAIN— ELK CREEK LOOP

A thrilling climb up the rugged 2,788-foot Elk Mountain, along a ridge with spectacular views, and down an old logging road that parallels the West Fork of Elk Creek.

Suggested
Maps
USGS Woods
Point and
Cochran
Quadrangles;
Wild Salmon
Center and
Outdoor
Project Wilson
River Map

Difficulty	Trailhead Coordinates
Strenuous	45.6100731, -123.4665833
Distance	Elevation
7.5 miles round-trip	2,800 feet elevation gain

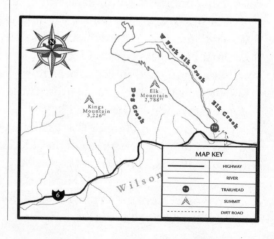

GETTING THERE

From Portland, drive west on US-26, then OR-6, toward Tillamook. Just past milepost 28, turn right into Elk Creek Campground and park in the lot near the end of the road.

Walk across the bridge and up the road until you see a trail to your left marked by a sign and a blue dot on a tree. Follow the trail to the top of a hill, where it becomes the new connector trail to the Kings Mountain Trailhead. Where the trail begins to level out, look for a tree on your right with a blue arrow also pointing right. Go through a slender notch in the rocks and pick up the narrow Elk Mountain trail.

Begin climbing steeply—you'll gain about 2,000 feet in the next 1.5 miles to the summit of Elk Mountain. You'll need to climb up the rocky trail, scale boulders, and contend with slippery hard-packed earth. The hike is more difficult on hot, dry days when there is no soft mud to give you traction. Be sure to wear sturdy shoes with a firm grip, as there are precarious cliffs at the edge of the trail.

At a grassy ledge at about 0.5 miles, you can take a breather and get a bird's-eye view of the Wilson River Highway snaking below you. In spring and early summer, this open area is dotted with wildflowers such as Indian paintbrush and yellow desert parsley. Past the ledge, the narrow trail resumes its steep ascent, occasionally passing over a "false summit" to descend briefly. To make the hike more rewarding and less grueling, stop often to take in the panoramic of the craggy rock faces and rugged peaks around you.

At about 2 miles, pass through a forested area with impressive snags left from the Tillamook Burn before you reach the summit—a grassy, wildflower-covered bluff. This excellent lunch spot rewards you with magnificent views of Kings Mountain to the west, Saddle Mountain to the north, and—if you're lucky—Tillamook Bay due west. Don't forget to sign the summit register before you continue the loop.

To resume the hike, look for a sign on a snag that says "Kings Mountain—3.4 miles, steep areas" and an arrow that points straight down. Here the trail takes a nosedive down the boulder-strewn far side of the mountain. Use extra caution on the descent, which is quite steep.

At about 2.25 miles, with the hardest part of the hike behind you, continue on a relatively flat trail under

Photo courtesy of T. J. Carter

cliffs covered with sedum, along a rock catwalk, and through high-elevation forest. Even in late spring, it's possible to encounter snow in the forested sections of the trail at this elevation; if there is snow, follow the blue dots on the trees. During mid-summer, look for tiger lilies blooming along the way.

At 2.75 miles, the trail joins a grassy old logging road on top of a flat ridge with expansive views. At about 3 miles, look for a T-intersection in the ridge-top trail. The left fork circles back to Kings Mountain. The wider roadbed to the right takes you to West Fork Elk Creek. In early summer, notice the alpine garden of pink phlox and purple penstemon at the fork.

Turn right and stay on the relatively flat roadbed, avoiding the steep road that veers up to the left. At about 3.75 miles, meet West Fork Elk Creek Road, which descends gently—but occasionally steeply—to Elk Creek Campground. The road, which was converted to a trail closed to all motor vehicles, passes by stands of maidenhair fern and mossy grottos. The final section parallels West Fork Elk Creek, where beaver live and winter steelhead spawn.

KINGS MOUNTAIN

7

This rigorous trek up Kings Mountain rewards hikers with the opportunity to savor the views of the ocean to the west, the Cascade peaks to the east, and the rolling mountain ranges of the Tillamook Forest all around.

Suggested Maps
ODF Tillamook State Forest Trail Guide: Kings Mountain, Elk Mountain, and Elk Creek Trails; Wild Salmon Center and Outdoor Project Wilson River Map

Difficulty
Strenuous

Distance
5.4 miles
round-trip

Trailhead Coordinates
45.5969, -123.5063

Elevation
2,450 feet
elevation gain

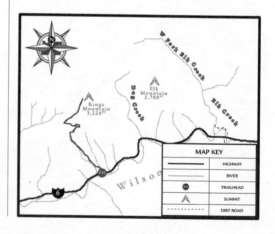

GETTING THERE

From Portland, drive west on US-26, then OR-6, toward Tillamook. Shortly past milepost 25, look for the Kings Mountain Trailhead, marked by a sign with a hiker symbol on the north side of the highway. Park in the parking area at the trailhead.

Walk up the Kings Mountain trail, marked by blue dots on the trees, through the second-growth forest with a lush understory. Here and there, poking through carpets of sorrel and ferns, you'll pass huge stumps remaining from the original old-growth forest. At about 0.25 miles, keep straight to where the Wilson River Trail branches right. A sign at 1 mile tells you you've reached 1,500 feet elevation. At 1.5 miles, another sign lets you know you've gained 500 more feet in half a mile. Continue climbing at a mostly steep grade, passing through open areas along the south-facing slopes of Kings Mountain that allow panoramic views of the Wilson River corridor and the coastal mountains to the southwest.

Keep straight and uphill, avoiding a trail that branches left and may be blocked. At 3,000 feet, you'll come to a small bench of land with a picnic table—a good place to take a break before the final push to the 3,226-foot summit. The rest of the climb will no longer be shaded but instead will be along an exposed rocky path lined with—depending on the season—wildflowers such as phlox, Indian paintbrush, penstemon, and asters. Notice the tall gray snags that tower over the new forest on the upper slopes of the mountain. These reminders of the Tillamook Burn more than half a century ago still have a niche in the forest ecosystem as nest sites for certain species of birds. At the summit, a meadow invites a well-deserved rest; use this opportunity to sign the summit register next to the trail. Take time to savor the views of the ocean to the west, the Cascade peaks to the east, and the rolling mountain ranges of the Tillamook Forest all around. When you're ready, retrace your steps to the trailhead.

Photo courtesy of
Riley Pittenger

ELK MOUNTAIN—KINGS MOUNTAIN TRAVERSE

8

A classic, challenging loop hike tagging the summits of both Elk and Kings Mountains, with wide ranging views along the way. Steep scrambling on rough, rocky trails required.

Difficulty	Trailhead Coordinates
Strenuous	45.59725, -123.506067
Distance	Elevation
10.7 miles	2,546 feet gain

Suggested Maps
ODF Tillamook State Forest Trail Guide: Kings Mountain, Elk Mountain, and Elk Creek Trails; Wild Salmon Center and Outdoor Project Wilson River Map

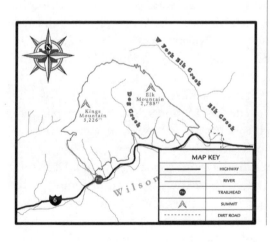

MAP KEY

————	HIGHWAY
	RIVER
🅣🅗	TRAILHEAD
⋀	SUMMIT
- - - - - -	DIRT ROAD

GETTING THERE

From Portland, drive west on US-26, then OR-6, toward Tillamook. Park at the Kings Mountain Trailhead on OR-6, 0.2 miles east of milepost 25. Hike up the Kings Mountain trail for 0.1 miles, to its intersection with the Wilson River Trail. Turn right, and follow the Wilson River Trail eastward, through mixed woodlands, skirting a small meadow and crossing several creeks along the way. Watch for a sign identifying the Elk Mountain trail at 3.5 miles; the sign is at the top of a small rise before the Wilson River Trail makes its final descent down to Elk Creek Campground. Turn left.

The first few steps up the Elk Mountain trail give the hiker a forewarning of the steep terrain to come, as the path rises 1,900 feet in the next 1.4 miles to the summit of Elk Mountain. Along the way, several precipitous drop-offs provide spectacular views of the Wilson River valley far below. Use caution, as the footing can be quite slippery in spots, especially during the summer months when there is no moist earth for traction.

After passing over a false summit, the top of Elk Mountain is reached at 4.9 miles. Sign the register, and enjoy the grand views of Kings Mountain just to the west. Continuing north, the path will have a short, very steep descent, demanding careful foot placements. Use your hands for balance. Thereafter, the trail becomes more moderate, passing under cliffs covered with moss, across a rocky catwalk, and down into a large flat area once used as a camp. Beyond the flat area, continue on an old logging trace past several long switchbacks to a high-country promenade with great views of nearby Kings Mountain and distant Cascade snow peaks.

At 6.9 miles, a major trail intersection is reached, with the Elk Mountain trail continuing on straight ahead to its junction with the Elk Creek trail and the Kings Mountain trail branching left. Take the Kings Mountain trail south, following an old roadbed for about 0.6 miles until it breaks into the open at the northern end of Kings Mountain. Savor the view of the Dog Creek valley below, then cross over to the precipitous west side of Kings Mountain. Here, you will soon traverse under huge cliffs and above several vertical drop-offs along the edge of the trail.

In spots, the trail becomes extremely steep and treacherous; a rope tied to a tree may be present at one point to assist those less sure of their footing. Finally, with the hardest scrambling behind you, the trail will climb steeply back up to a small meadow just north of the Kings Mountain summit. Soon, the summit register is reached, and expansive views open up to the west and south, including a glimpse of the Pacific Ocean far to the southwest. When ready, descend the final 2.5 miles down the Kings Mountain trail to the trailhead on OR-6.

KINGS MOUNTAIN JUNIOR

9

Can be used as an alternative route to the summit of Kings Mountain, providing unique views of its western face.

Suggested
Maps
ODF
Tillamook
State Forest
Trail Guide:
Kings
Mountain, Elk
Mountain,
and Elk
Creek Trails;
Wild Salmon
Center and
Outdoor
Project Wilson
River Map

Difficulty	Trailhead Coordinates
Moderate, with one short, very steep section	45.5969, -123.5063

Distance	Elevation
3.4 miles round-trip	1,690 feet elevation gain

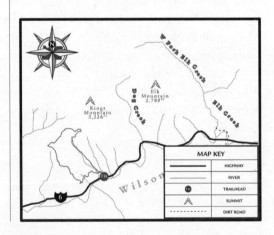

MAP KEY

	HIGHWAY
	RIVER
	TRAILHEAD
	SUMMIT
	DIRT ROAD

GETTING THERE

From Portland, drive west on US-26, then OR-6, toward Tillamook. Start at the Kings Mountain Trailhead on OR-6, 0.2 miles east of milepost 25. Hike up the Kings Mountain trail for 0.1 miles to its intersection with the Wilson River Trail. Turn left and follow the Wilson River Trail gradually uphill for the next 1.9 miles, passing through mixed woodlands and crossing a small bridge over a stream at 0.6 miles from the trailhead. As the trail levels out in an alder grove at 2 miles, watch for an unmarked path rising steeply to the right—here the Wilson River Trail begins to swing to the north. Turn right here and climb steeply uphill on this trail for the next 0.2 miles—a descent by this route is not recommended during the dry season when there is no soft earth to keep your boots from sliding. As the grade finally eases near the top, watch for a sign on a tree to your left, which identifies the route you have just climbed as the "Coronary Ridge."

Photo courtesy of Riley Pittenger

Walk along the ridge path, enjoying expansive views of the Wilson River valley and the secluded west face of nearby Kings Mountain. Be careful of loose rock along the eroded edge in a few places. Once you have passed the unmarked summit, the trail will descend steeply to the northeast, then regain elevation to join the main Kings Mountain trail approximately 0.7 miles below its summit. To finish the hike, turn right here and follow the well-traveled path back down to your car. Or, if you are still feeling fresh, a left turn will take you up to the main Kings Mountain summit.

Photo courtesy of Riley Pittenger

LARCH MOUNTAIN—
BELL CAMP ROAD

10

A pleasant walk on private forest roads to a high point in the eastern Tillamook forest that provides unique views of Saddle Mountain and the Salmonberry River Canyon.

Difficulty
Moderate

Distance
6.2 miles round-trip

Trailhead Coordinates
45.667417, -123.40295

Elevation
Approximately 600 feet
elevation gain

GETTING THERE

From Portland, drive west on US-26 until you reach Timber Junction, and take Timber Road south into the small village of Timber. Turn right onto Cochran Road and follow it into the forest for 3.8 miles to the junction with Round Top Road (1.3 miles past the Reheer's Camp Trailhead). Turn left and follow Round Top Road, which will wind gradually uphill past several marked and unmarked intersections until it finally straightens out and becomes Bell Camp Road at 3.9 miles (7.7 miles in from Timber). Stay on Bell Camp Road for

Suggested
Maps
Wild Salmon
Center and
Outdoor
Project Wilson
River Map

another 2.6 miles to its junction with Standard Grade, then go straight for another 0.2 miles to a parking area over-looking a massive clearcut above the Salmonberry River canyon. Park your car here.

Head south on foot along Standard Grade, passing through a yellow gate and continuing on for 2 miles to the intersection with Storey Burn Road. Turn right and continue straight (west) on Standard Grade for just over 0.5 miles. When you see SG106 coming in sharply from the left at milepost 7, turn onto this smaller lane and follow it steeply uphill. In 0.4 miles, SG106 will flatten out briefly and bend sharply right; 0.1 miles further you will come to a "Y" intersection. Taking the right fork will lead in another

0.1 miles to the rocky Larch Mountain summit, with views to the east of Round Top and several Cascade snow peaks, while the left offers views of the south-ern and western Tillamook Forest, including nearby Elk and Kings Mountains. Retrace your steps to return to your car.

Photo courtesy of Chris Smith

LARCH MOUNTAIN—
STOREY BURN ROAD

11

*An alternative eastern approach to Larch
Mountain that is shorter than the Bell Camp
Road hike. Hikers will enjoy great views of several
Cascade peaks.*

Difficulty	Trailhead Coordinates
Moderate	45.668760, -123.403624

Distance	Elevation
4.2 miles	Approximately 600 feet
round-trip	elevation gain

GETTING THERE

From Portland, drive west on US-26, then
OR-6, toward Tillamook. Turn off OR-6 at
milepost 33, into the large parking/staging
area north of the highway. Well-marked
Storey Burn Road begins at the west end of
this parking area. Follow Storey Burn Road
for 5.3 miles to a small parking area at the
top of a hill about 0.1 miles before a large
yellow gate. Leave your car here. Do not
drive through the gate, even if it is open; it
may be locked when you return.

Suggested
Maps
Wild Salmon
Center and
Outdoor
Project Wilson
River Map

Walk through the gate and follow Storey Burn Road for another mile, where it will intersect with Standard Grade. Continue straight (west) on Standard Grade for just over 0.5 miles. When you see SG106 coming in sharply from the left at milepost 7, turn onto this smaller lane and follow it steeply uphill. In 0.4 miles, SG106 will flatten out briefly and bend sharply right; 0.1 miles further you will come to a "Y" intersection. Taking the right fork for another 0.1 miles will lead to the rocky Larch Mountain summit, with views to the east of Round Top and several Cascade snow peaks, while the left offers views of the southern and western Tillamook Forest, including nearby Elk and Kings Mountains. Retrace your steps to return to your car.

Photo courtesy of Chris Smith

EAST STANDARD GRADE ROAD

12

A straightforward hike, bike, or winter ski outing on a gently rolling forest road with expansive views along much of the route. Best traveled on weekends, as the road can be quite busy with logging traffic during the week. The entire route is on private timberland, so take extra care to give right-of-way to any traffic you may encounter.

Difficulty Moderate, but long	**Trailhead Coordinates** 45.667417, -123.40295
Distance 23 miles round-trip to the West Gate; 21.8 miles round-trip to Blue Lake	**Elevation** 300 feet to the West Gate; an additional 700 feet lost, then regained on the trip to Blue Lake

Suggested Maps 2012 Northwest Oregon Protection District Map

GETTING THERE
From Portland, drive west on US-26, then OR-6, toward Tillamook. Turn off OR-6 at milepost 33, into the large gravel parking/staging area north of the highway. Storey Burn Road is well-marked and begins at the west end of this parking area. Follow Storey Burn for 5.3 miles, as it climbs

gradually to a small parking area at the top of a hill on the left, about 0.1 miles before a large yellow gate. Leave your car here, but do not drive through the gate. Even if it's open when you get there, it may be locked when you return.

Walk or bike through the gate and head west on Storey Burn Road for another mile until it intersects with Standard Grade. Continue straight (west) on Standard Grade as it rises gently for another 4 miles to its intersection with Elk Creek Road and then descends again to an intersection with the North Fork Wilson River Road at 10.1 miles. Along the way, enjoy expansive views of the Tillamook Forest and distant peaks to the north and south.

One section in particular, about 6 miles from the gate, offers an unrivaled panorama from the west coastal mountains, past Saddle Mountain, past Rainier and St. Helens, all the way east to Mt. Adams. From the North Wilson River Road intersection, you can either stay on the level for another 1.4 miles, following Standard Grade to its west end gate, or you can take a sharp left onto North Fork Wilson River Road, which will soon lead you steeply downhill for 0.8 miles to Blue Lake. If you take the second option, watch for a faint trail leading down through the woods, just after passing by the lake, and take this down to the shore. Retrace your route to return to the car.

NOTE

If conditions are just right in the winter—and there has been significant snowfall down to an elevation of about 2,500 feet—it may be possible to drive up to or near the parking lot at the top of Storey Burn Road (four-wheel drive recommended) and enjoy a day of backcountry skiing along Standard Grade.

Photo courtesy of Chris Smith

13

WEST STANDARD GRADE ROAD TO BLUE LAKE

Suggested
Maps
2012
Northwest
Oregon
Protection
District Map

A pleasant hike along forest roads to a secluded lake located on private land deep in the heart of the Tillamook State Forest. Four-wheel drive is recommended to reach the trailhead.

Difficulty	**Trailhead Coordinates**
Easy	45.683333, -123.566667
Distance	**Elevation**
4.4 miles round-trip	750 feet loss, then gain

GETTING THERE

From Portland, drive west on US-26, then OR-6, toward Tillamook. From milepost 23 on OR-6, go west a short distance to the Jones Creek Campground entrance and the Diamond Mill off-highway vehicle (OHV) area. Turn north on this road and cross the river. At 0.3 miles, turn right toward Diamond Mill, following this road past the OHV staging area to an intersection at 1.8 miles. Take the road to the right and continue on along the West Fork of the Wilson River, passing roads exiting to the right across bridges at 3.1 and 4.1 miles. At 5 miles, there will be a third exit to the right;

turn here and cross over the unmarked bridge. Follow this steep, rough road uphill until you reach another fork in the road at 8.7 miles. Turn right here and continue on for an additional 1.6 miles, where you will finally intersect with Cook Creek Road just before its name changes to Standard Grade. Park along the side of the road and walk to the gate.

Walk around one end of the heavy metal gate and stroll along the pleasant, level road, now in private forestland. At 0.6 miles, you will come to a major crossroad and the beginning of expansive views of the northern Tillamook State Forest. Continue straight for another 0.8 miles to a second crossroad and take the right fork. About 0.3 miles further, this road will split. Take the left fork, heading downhill at a moderate grade, until you see Blue Lake through the trees to your left. Just after passing by the lake, find a faint trail on the left leading down to the shore. Although the surrounding forest was clearcut in 2001, alders have grown back tall enough around the lake to give it at least some feeling of seclusion again.

Retrace your steps to return to the trailhead.

Photo courtesy of Brian Pasko

KEENIG CREEK TO FOOTBRIDGE

14

This is the lowest section of the Wilson River Trail. It is a misnomer to call it the Wilson River because it actually traverses the slopes high above the river. However, it is a beautiful, nicely graded opportunity for a peaceful forest hike. It is best done as a car shuttle, since the last piece is a drop of 1,500 feet in 1.5 miles, which would make for a long day if done as an out-and-back.

Suggested
Maps
ODF
Tillamook
State Forest
Trail Guide:
Wilson River
Trail; Wild
Salmon
Center and
Outdoor
Project Wilson
River Map

Difficulty	Trailhead Coordinates
Moderate	45.5418777, -123.6126709
Distance	Elevation
6.1 miles one-way	Approximately 1,500 feet gain

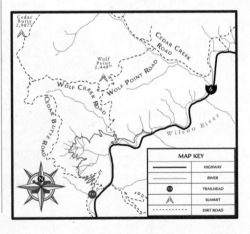

GETTING THERE

Drive both cars to the Keenig Creek Trailhead. To get there from Portland, drive on OR-6 to milepost 18 and turn right (north) at Cedar Butte Road. Drive over the bridge and immediately turn left on Muesial Creek Road. Keep your eyes peeled as it is a small, unobtrusive sign. Continue 0.2 miles and park at the trailhead. Do not assume that you should park at the Keenig Campground sign; this is a fire lane parking area. The trailhead is just beyond. Leave one car here and drive back to the Footbridge Day Use Area at milepost 20 to park the second car. The parking area is just below the road.

Follow the trail at the southwest corner of the parking area up to the road and continue west for a short distance until you reach stairs that lead down to Footbridge. Cross the bridge to admire the river and then continue on a faint trail for a few hundred yards across the rocks to where a well-marked trail begins in the woods. Follow this a short distance to a junction with the main Wilson River Trail.

Turn left (west) and follow the trail for a mile as it climbs steadily and then drops to Wolf Creek Road. Turn right onto Wolf Creek Road and, after a short distance, pick up the trail on the other side of the road as it drops to Wolf Creek. Cross a side creek and Wolf Creek via the log bridges. This is a beautiful area of mixed forest, flowers, and cliffs—a great lunch spot for a shorter hike.

On the other side of the creek, climb steadily on a well-graded trail for about a mile to a ridge and then continue traversing a beautiful, mostly level trail along steep hillsides with occasional forest vistas for about 2.5 miles. In less dry conditions, several creeks and waterfalls will cross this part of the trail. However, if you take the trail during dry conditions, such as at the end of August, the creeks are mostly dry or trickling, and most flowers have died—although there are still yellow monkey flowers and you may hear juncos, robins, or woodpeckers. Several of the creeks are bordered by large stumps, which serve as evidence of the old-growth trees that were cut to make way for the trail. The forest is now an open mix of mainly deciduous trees. As always in an area of steep drop offs, be prepared for trail damage and loose rocks, especially after heavy rain.

Photo courtesy of Riley Pittenger

The trail then intersects with a gravel road (Cedar Butte Road). Turn left (downhill), and in 50 yards reconnect with the trail on the right. In the next 1.5 miles, the trail drops steadily for 1,500 feet to the trailhead, with numerous switchbacks. This portion of the trail was clearcut in the past and is much more open than the higher part of the trail that is filled with lots of shrubs and some deciduous trees.

JONES CREEK DAY USE AREA TO FOOTBRIDGE

15

A beautiful hike along the best-known part of the Wilson River Trail, including Wilson Falls and a visit to the rebuilt bridge at the site of the old stone footbridge.

Difficulty
Easy

Distance
7 miles round-trip

Trailhead Coordinates
45.588455, -123.555214

Elevation
About 500 feet gain along rolling terrain

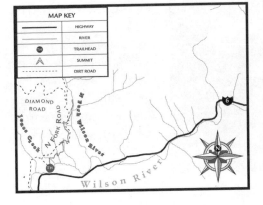

Suggested Maps
ODF Tillamook State Forest Trail Guide: Wilson River Trail; Wild Salmon Center and Outdoor Project Wilson River Map

GETTING THERE

You can access the trail from the Jones Creek Day Use Area or from the Tillamook Forest Visitor Center, but be aware that access to the trail from the visitor center is only an option when the center is open and that it currently closes at 5 p.m.

To reach the Jones Creek Trailhead, drive west on OR-6. Between mileposts 22 and 23 turn to the right at a sign for Jones Creek Campground/Smith Homestead. Cross a bridge and immediately turn left into the parking lot for the Jones Creek Day Use Area.

Take one of the short trails from the parking area toward the river and pick up the Wilson River Trail. Turn right and

follow the well-marked trail to the end of the day use area and then to a bridge that crosses Jones Creek. As you walk, look for huge plant-encrusted stumps that are a reminder of the size of the old-growth trees that originally lined the river. A few hundred yards after Jones Creek, you will come to a palatial bridge crossing the river to the Visitor Center

Photo courtesy of Chris Smith

entrance. (If you are accessing the trail at the Visitor Center, park there and either access the bridge through the Center or by one of the side trails from the parking lot.) An information sign at the bridge says 0.8 miles to Cedar Creek, 1.7 to Wilson Falls, and 3.2 to Footbridge.

Continue west along a beautiful part of the river, with several side trails down to picnic spots and swimming holes. The trail meets Cedar Creek Road, drops back into the trees, and then meets the road again to cross Cedar Creek. Watch carefully for signs as the trail meets and leaves the road. At about 1.4 miles, the trail leaves the river and climbs steadily to Wilson Falls. This is a good turning point if you don't want to go all the way to Footbridge. Be sure to look up. The streamflow dwindles in summer, but the height of the falls is still impressive.

From the falls, continue to a bend looking down on the river and then descend gradually to a signed junction at 3.5 miles. For a considerably longer hike, possibly including a car shuttle, you can continue straight for another 6 miles to the end of the Wilson River Trail at Keenig Creek. To get to Footbridge, turn left at the junction and follow a steep trail down to a stony beach and up to a sandy ridge with cliffs lining a gorge. Stand on it and watch the beautiful deep green river. There are several popular swimming spots in summer, and at other seasons it is a good place to look for salmon making their slow way upstream.

Unless you have parked a car at the parking lot for the bridge, return the way you came.

JONES CREEK TO DIAMOND MILL

16

This short section of the Wilson River Trail starts near an excellent picnic area along the Wilson River and climbs up to the North Fork of the Wilson River. This trail comes close to a popular off-highway vehicle recreation area, but the vehicles do not share the trail with hikers.

Difficulty	Trailhead Coordinates
Easy	45.5895, -123.5563
Distance	Elevation
1.9 miles one-way	200 feet gain

Suggested
Maps
ODF
Tillamook
State Forest
Trail Guide:
Wilson River
Trail; Wild
Salmon Center
and Outdoor
Project Wilson
River Map

GETTING THERE

From Portland, drive west on US-26 and OR-6. Just past milepost 23, take a right at the sign for Jones Creek Day Use Area and Diamond Mill OHV staging area. Stay left and cross the bridge, then turn left into the parking area for Jones Creek Day Use Area.

The start of the trail is back across the road, east of the parking lot. Soon after you start, you'll see a trail leading to the equestrian trailhead off to the left. Continue straight

Photo courtesy of T. J. Carter

along the trail, which will start to go uphill slightly. Enjoy the forest of second-growth hemlock and alders. You'll encounter a small stream after about a quarter mile, and the trail will go up at a steeper clip. At about 0.75 miles, the trail crosses the road. Simply follow the sign on the other side of the road to resume the trail. Follow the trail up through several switchbacks and cross the road again after another 0.5 miles. At this point you may hear ATVs or motorbikes nearby. They do not share the trail with hikers. Follow the trail down some switchbacks about 100 feet. You'll see a culvert to your left, and shortly thereafter a trail leading up to the Diamond Mill OHV staging area. Stay on the main trail along the edge of the staging area. You should hear the river on your right. Continue around the edge of the staging area until you arrive at a large foot-bridge across the river. Across the footbridge, the Wilson River Trail continues toward Kings Mountain. Return the way you came to your vehicle.

KINGS MOUNTAIN TO DIAMOND MILL

17

This fun and accessible hike links the Diamond Mill OHV staging area with the Kings Mountain Trailhead and follows the Wilson River Trail around several bluffs with beautiful views of the Wilson River Corridor. This hike is an excellent choice for a half-day shuttle or for linking with other Wilson River Trail hikes for longer, more strenuous hikes. Be aware that many mountain bikers use this trail as part of longer rides from the Kings Mountain and Elk Mountain Trailheads, and the bikers do not always make themselves known as they descend around blind corners and switchbacks.

Suggested
Maps
ODF
Tillamook
State Forest
Trail Guide:
Wilson River
Trail; Wild
Salmon
Center and
Outdoor
Project Wilson
River Map

Difficulty	Trailhead Coordinates
Moderate to strenuous	45.596994, -123.506440

Distance	Elevation
5.5 miles one-way	1,400 feet gain

GETTING THERE

KINGS MOUNTAIN TRAILHEAD
Take US-26 west from Portland, then exit to OR-6 toward Tillamook. Follow OR-6

along the Wilson River until you reach the Kings Mountain Trailhead on the right between mileposts 25 and 26.

DIAMOND MILL OHV STAGING AREA

If you take the shuttle option, drop one car at Diamond Mill and the other at Kings Mountain. To get to Diamond Mill, follow the instructions for Kings Mountain but continue a few miles on OR-6 past the Kings Mountain Trailhead to Jones Creek Day Use Area and Diamond Mill OHV staging area on the right, just past milepost 23. Follow the road north across the bridge until you reach the four-way intersection of dirt roads and a sign indicating the Diamond Mill OHV staging area. Take a right and follow the dirt road uphill as it curves around several ridges providing a rising view of the Wilson River corridor to the south with several small turnouts on the right side of the road for passing trucks. After approximately 2 miles, you will see a sign for the Diamond Mill OHV staging area. Note that the fees are only for off-highway vehicle use and overnight camping.

Beginning from the Kings Mountain parking lot, follow the trail north for 0.1 miles to the intersection of Kings Mountain trail with the Wilson River Trail. Turn left at the trail junction and follow the Wilson River Trail to the west. The climb from the trailhead becomes fairly steep as the trail wraps north away from the Wilson River. Keep an eye out for muddy sections in early spring or fall. After some switchbacks and a climbing grade, you will come across great views of the Wilson River corridor to the left as the trail takes you up and around stunning rock bluffs and more southern views over the next 2.5 miles. In the gullies between ridges, you will cross several small streams that will be dry or trickles in late summer.

The trail begins to decline steeply at first, leading to a moderate decline with several switchbacks into the valley through a beautiful section of fern groves and high pines with moss-filled meadows and underbrush. The trail will intersect with an overgrown logging road that switchbacks across the trail several times and disappears to the south as you descend. On weekends, you may hear the sound of distant ATVs and dirtbikes as you approach the Diamond Mill OHV staging area. At the bottom of the hill there will be a large, wooden footbridge crossing over a clear pool of water and some nice beaches that make for an excellent lunch break or post-hike rest.

Go back the way you came to Kings Mountain, follow the sign toward the staging area to collect your shuttle, or continue along the Wilson River Trail to the southwest, which links to the Jones Creek Day Use Area and other Wilson River hikes to the west.

Photo courtesy of Riley Pittenger

ELK CREEK TO KINGS MOUNTAIN

18

Suggested
Maps
ODF
Tillamook
State Forest
Trail Guide:
Wilson River
Trail, Wild
Salmon
Center and
Outdoor
Project Wilson
River Map

This well-maintained section of the Wilson River Trail runs from the Elk Creek Campground to the Kings Mountain Trailhead. Most of the time it's several hundred feet above the river, traversing steeply forested slopes and crossing several creeks. It can be done as an out-and-back or a one-way with a car shuttle. Weather permitting, this is a good option for a winter hike. Besides the section of the Wilson River Trail, there's a whole network of trails in this area that can be combined into hikes of varying difficulties.

Difficulty	Trailhead Coordinates
Easy to Moderate	45.6040286, -123.5500879

Distance	Elevation
3.6 miles one-way	200 feet gain

GETTING THERE

Take OR-6 to the entrance of Elk Creek Campground opposite milepost 28. Turn into the campground. If the campground is closed, park at the parking area close to the highway and walk from there. Otherwise, drive 0.25 miles to a new parking area just beyond the campground.

Photo courtesy of Bruce Couch

Just beyond the parking area, find the Wilson River Trailhead on the left. Hike uphill for 0.2 miles to a junction with the trail to Elk Mountain, which climbs steeply to the right and has options for a variety of routes in the area. The Wilson River Trail continues to climb and then evens out under a line of rocky crags before running parallel to the river well below. Note the varied colors of lichens on the rocks, including bright red "British Soldiers." Cross several small creeks and descend steeply to a bridge over Dog Creek at 2 miles. From Dog Creek, climb again and then descend to traverse above several small meadows. You'll reach the junction with the Kings Mountain trail at 3.5 miles. Turn left for 0.1 miles to reach the highway, or return the way you came.

Elk may be grazing in the meadows, and you're likely to find elk scat on the trail. Even in mid-March, look for woodland flowers including yellow violets and coltsfoot.

LITTLE NORTH FORK OF THE WILSON (LOWER RIVER TRAIL)

19

A secluded but very reachable hike on an unimproved but generally level trail that follows the Little North Fork of the Wilson River.

Difficulty
Easy

Distance
3 miles round-trip,
with optional trail
extensions

Trailhead Coordinates
45.4840836, -123.7256761

Elevation
150 feet gain

GETTING THERE

From Portland, drive west on US-26, then OR-6 to the trailhead between mileposts 6 and 5. Park outside the yellow gate just east of Mills Bridge on the north side of the highway. During deer and elk hunting season in the fall, the gate is open for hunters to drive through.

Start at the gate and walk along Rush Road, an ODF road. After 0.5 miles, the road widens, curves to the right, and heads uphill. Look for a former left fork (actually

Suggested
Maps
Wild Salmon
Center and
Outdoor
Project Wilson
River Map

Rush Road), now blocked by rocks and fallen trees. Walk around this obstacle to find a narrow footpath along the old roadbed. *(See Trail Option 1 below.)* Follow the footpath upstream along the river through damp, shady woods for about a mile. Along most of the path, the slope down to the river is rather steep, although there are a few rough access routes used by fishermen. You may also notice some steps down to the stream near the beginning of the trail.

The trail ends at a wide, shady spot in the river that's said to be a prime winter steelhead drift. This would be a good place to picnic and swim before heading back. Look for a notable colony of maidenhair ferns growing on a dripping ledge just north of trail's end. *(See Trail Option 2 below.)*

Photo courtesy of Guido Rahr

TRAIL OPTIONS

1. The well-maintained road that goes uphill from the first fork (Ming Point Road) is another potential hike that can be easily done in conjunction with this one. There's a good overlook of the Little North Fork about 0.75 miles past the fork. Ming Point is 2 miles from the fork.

2. At certain times of the year, you could—with appropriate footwear—extend your trip by walking directly in the stream. Wading through wide, shallow pools will reward you with beautiful views of the river as it bends sharply west and its banks steepen. About 0.5 miles up the river, you can see a patch of old-growth trees that escaped the woodcutter's saw. Many thanks to outdoorsmen Karl Konecky, Gene McMullen, and Guy Orcutt, who convinced the Bureau of Land Management (BLM) to acquire this stand.

3. About 7 miles up the Little North Fork from its confluence with the Wilson River, a short, lovely trail down to the stream descends for 1 to 2 miles to the Little North Fork canyon. The trail passes through abundant spring wildflowers and ends at a wide pool that may have been created by the piles of logs left at the former log staging area. If you pick your way across the logs, you can follow well-defined elk trails along the stream in a wide, flat canyon—a prime summer picnic area. Generally, you can walk to where the canyon narrows with steep rock walls. However, in the dry season, you can continue walking directly in the stream, where necessary, to the lower

Little North Fork trail about 5 miles downstream. This is a particularly scenic, unspoiled area of the Tillamook Forest. Access to the Gorge Road trail is via Coast Range Road or Muesial Creek Road; a four-wheel drive vehicle is strongly recommended.

TRIANGULATION POINT

If you have the legs for it, this is one of the best hikes in the Tillamook. The route leads to rarely traveled forest roads, climbing to an unobstructed viewpoint deep in the heart of the forest. May be done as an out-and-back hike, or as a longer loop version, which includes a stop at Kilchis Falls.

20

Suggested
Maps
USGS
Nehalem River
Quadrangle

Difficulty	Trailhead Coordinates
Strenuous	45.617833, -123.684417

Distance	Elevation
10 miles round-trip, or a 13.7-mile loop	Up to 2,400 feet gain

GETTING THERE

From the town of Tillamook, proceed north on US-101. Go 0.6 miles beyond the Tillamook Cheese Factory, then take a right onto Alderbrook Loop Road where a sign points toward the Kilchis River. Pass through the small village of Alderbrook and turn right where the road forks after about a mile. Go 1.2 miles further and turn right across a small bridge onto Kilchis Forest Road. Follow this well-maintained gravel road for just over 14 miles and find a place to park along the side of the road, near where Middle Road branches off to the left.

Hike steeply up Middle Road, gaining 1,300 feet in elevation in the first 1.5 miles. Watch for the first views of your objectives: the double-summited Triangulation Point off to the right at 1 mile and the north side of the Sawtooth Ridge shortly thereafter. At a four-way intersection just shy of 3 miles, take the right fork onto FB3. This will descend slightly before ascending again toward the point.

At 4.4 miles, take the left fork at the next intersection and follow this up to the saddle (a small dip in the land) between the north and south summits of Triangulation Point. Although the north summit is a few feet higher, we do not recommend going there since the views are limited and a satellite installation emits radiofrequency waves "unsafe for the general public," according to a sign posted there. Instead hike up to the open south summit for expansive views on all sides. If the sky is clear, look for the ghost of Mt. Hood floating just above the south shoulder of Kings Mountain to the east and a glimpse of the Pacific Ocean to the west. Although the occasional OHV may visit the point, you're likely to have the summit all to yourself if you avoid the busy holiday weekends.

From the south summit, you can retrace your steps to complete the out-and-back hike, or take the first road to the left as you begin your descent to continue on the loop option. This rough road will contour around to the west and then south of the south summit, reaching a five-way intersection in 0.5 miles. Cut straight across the intersection, ignoring the two branches which angle sharply backwards to the left and right, and take the right fork, heading

Photo courtesy of Chris Smith

downhill on Cedar Butte Road. Follow this route south for the next 2.7 miles. At the foot of Cedar Butte, turn right onto Kilchis Forest Road and follow this back to your car. Shortly after passing by 100-foot Kilchis Falls on your left, you'll be serenaded by the nearby Kilchis River for the final 2 miles of your hike.

Illustration courtesy of Lori LaBissoniere

TRASK-TUALATIN DRAINAGE

HENRY HAGG LAKE

A family-oriented, man-made lake near Forest Grove that features pleasant hiking and mountain biking trails through the woods and meadows along its shores. The lake was created by the damming of Scoggins Creek, which has its headwaters in the forest. In addition to recreation opportunities for nearby urban areas, the lake provides water to several communities. Park facilities include picnic tables, barbecues, restrooms, an accessible fishing pier, and a boat ramp (rental boats available at the C-Ramp Recreation Area). See http://www.co.washington. or.us/Support_Services/Facilities/Parks/ Hagglake for more information.

21

Difficulty	Trailhead Coordinates
Easy to Moderate	45.47667, -123.197442
Distance	Elevation
Up to 14.5 miles	500 feet gain

Suggested Maps
Washington County Henry Hagg Lake Map

GETTING THERE

From Portland, drive west on OR-8 (Tualatin Valley Highway) through Hillsboro to its junction with OR-47 on the outskirts of Forest Grove. Turn left (south) onto OR-47. After about 6 miles, turn right at signs for

Hagg Lake and Scoggins Valley. Continue about 3.5 more miles to the park entrance just before Scoggins Dam. A parking fee of $7 ($5 for seniors 55+ and veterans) is collected at the entrance booth. Depending on where you choose to hike, continue around the lake's perimeter road to the appropriate trailhead.

A hiking and mountain biking trail parallels the road most of the way around the Hagg Lake. At the points where Scoggins Creek, Tanner Creek, and Sain Creek enter the lake, there is no trail. You can either bushwhack or use the road. Additionally, there is an approximately 1.5-mile section over the dam and west of it where you must walk along the road.

Photo courtesy of Chris Smith

POSSIBLE HIKES INCLUDE

- **Lake Loop.** The trail undulates gently and is broken in a few spots near the perimeter road. Pass through varied terrain including woods, grasslands, and wetlands. This may take longer than you expect if conditions are wet (and muddy in spots). The trail is easy to follow in the heavily used southeastern half of the lake, but the northwestern half is narrower and at times difficult to distinguish from the abundance of social trails made by hikers and not supported by the park system, especially at the Fender's Blue Trailhead. To circle the entire lake is about 14.5 miles total.

- **Interpretive Trail.** Head north from Eagle Point Recreation Area to a short interpretive trail and return on the Lake Loop Trail in under a mile.

- **Eagle Point Recreation Area to Dam Overlook.** Hike about 2 miles round-trip through woods along the lakeshore. A good hike for families.

- **Fender's Blue to Osprey Point.** This hike is about 4 miles round-trip. Pass through a mix of woods and grassland and enjoy beautiful views of the lake. You'll have lots of opportunities for bird watching and plant identification. Portions of the grassland are designated "Eco-Sensitive Areas" in an effort to protect the plant Kincaid's lupine, which is host to the endangered Fender's blue butterfly. This part of the lake has a no-wake policy for motorized boats and is quieter in the summer than the southeast end near the dam. Picnic tables are available near Osprey Point. Be careful to stay on the designated trail.

- **Sain Creek Picnic Area.** Walk in either direction from this beautiful picnic area with shady sites overlooking an arm of the lake. Walk to the C-Ramp Recreation Area (0.5 miles) or along the southwest side of the lake as far as you like (watch out for flying discs as you pass through the disc golf course).
- **Cedar Grove to Tanner Creek.** This is another trail that's about 4 miles round-trip. A lovely mix of shady woods and grassland, this stretch is home to several picnic tables built for an Eagle Scout project in 2008. This is a great destination for a short hike and picnic.

Wherever you hike at the lake—especially in the areas farther from picnicking and boating activity—watch for signs of wildlife such as deer, elk, and coyotes. Woodland and meadow wildflowers are common in spring and summer. Fall and winter bring a wide variety of birds, including bald eagles, ospreys, and several varieties of owls. A good place for birding is the stretch of trail from the C-Ramp Recreation Area to Scoggins Creek. Look for ducks and shorebirds as well as sapsuckers in the trees along the trail.

THE PENINSULA TRAIL

A short, scenic, and occasionally steep trail along a finger of land inside a hairpin bend of the Trask River, leading to a rare stand of old-growth conifers. A great place to have a picnic and perhaps swim or fish in the river below. The Trask River is a beautiful and largely undeveloped fishery with large, abundant pools and spectacular basalt rock formations. The river has significant runs of wild steelhead, wild sea-run cutthroat trout, and both fall and spring chinook. Suitable for older children.

22

Difficulty	Trailhead Coordinates
Easy	45.4555, -123.6717

Distance	Elevation
1 mile round-trip	About 100 feet gain

Suggested Maps USGS Peninsula Quadrangle topographic map

GETTING THERE

From Portland, drive west on US-26, then OR-6, toward Tillamook. Watch the mileposts indicating the remaining distance to Tillamook. About 3 miles before Tillamook (about a mile after the Wilson River Canyon opens up into a flood plain), turn left at a sign for Trask River Road; this actually puts you on Olson Road. Follow this road for about 2 miles and turn left at another sign for Trask River Road just before a bridge over the Trask River. Watch for The Peninsula Park between mileposts 7 and 8 on the south side of the road. Park in the small lot with the "Hiking Trail" sign.

Start the hike near a large Department of Forestry sign on the left side of the parking area. You'll climb steeply at first, then follow a narrow ridge. At the first open spot, make sure to stop and take in the view of the river and the Coast Range in the distance.

Photo courtesy of Chris Smith

Continuing on the trail, you'll encounter more short, steep sections with steps to help you up or down. When you reach a fork where the trail starts a loop, stay left. At 0.5 miles from the trailhead, come to a stand of old-growth trees, including hemlock, western redcedar, and Sitka spruce. Here you'll find good picnic sites, some with wooden tables and fire pits. A short walk to the river leads to a calm pool that could be a fine place to swim on a hot day. However, use caution, as there are rapids and logs downstream. The shoreline ranges from sandy beach to gravel to volcanic rock.

To return, retrace your steps or continue on the loop trail back to the fork where you previously turned left. Again, keep left to reach the trailhead.

Trask County Park, a few miles up the road from the Peninsula, offers camping, toilets, and a boat launch. Due to river hazards, boating below the Peninsula is not recommended.

GOLD PEAK

23

Gold Peak (2,847 feet) is one of the high points in the Trask Valley east of Tillamook. An easy road walk for most of the way but with a short but difficult off-trail climb to the top. Great views of the forest on the way and 360-degree view from the mainly forested summit. Note: This is an active logging area. Drive carefully and be on the lookout for logging trucks; four-wheel drive is necessary for steep parts. A CB radio is helpful.

Suggested
Maps
2012
Northwest
Oregon
Protection
District Map

Difficulty	Trailhead Coordinates
Moderate to strenuous	45.423351, -123.641514

Distance	Elevation
2 to 10 miles round-trip, depending where you park. Recommended route is to a ridge before the summit, 3 miles round-trip	500 to 2,400 feet gain, depending on where you park. Recommended route about 500 feet

GETTING THERE

From Portland, drive west on US-26, then OR-6, toward Tillamook. Once on OR-6, drive west from Banks toward Tillamook. As you near Tillamook, look for the milepost 3 sign, then for a green sign on the highway pointing toward Trask River Road. Turn left at the sign that reads Olson Road; after approximately 0.1 miles, Olson Road becomes Trask River Road. Continue on Trask River Road for about 2 miles, then look for a green sign indicating a left turn to stay on Trask River Road. Turn left and continue for 11.7 miles to Trask County Park. There are restrooms here and an informational sign about the historic Trask Toll Road.

From Trask County Park, continue another 1.5 miles along Trask River Road to a one-lane bridge across the south fork of the Trask River. Here the road turns to gravel. Also note a warning sign about active logging in the area. There is a CB channel indicated, so if you have a CB radio you can listen for logging trucks coming down the road.

Photo courtesy of Brian Pasko

Continue on the gravel road as it winds for a mile along the river to the Hollywood Staging Area. Just past the staging area, turn right onto Edwards Creek Road. After 0.3 miles, hook right onto Gold Peak Road. From here, the road is steep uphill on fairly rough gravel, best with four-wheel drive. Continue on Gold Peak Road for 2.5 miles to the intersection with Stone Road. There is a wide spot in the road here with good places to park off the shoulder.

Recommended route: Park here and continue on foot uphill along Gold Peak Road. This is a well-maintained, single-lane gravel road with views out across the forest and lots of spring flowers—lupine, bleeding heart, corydalis, and many others. After about a mile, you'll come to a spur road on the right. This road leads about 0.5 miles along a ridge with good views of Gold Peak and the surrounding valleys. It's easy walking, only some of it uphill. It ends in a gravel lot/turnaround. To return, retrace your steps.

Optional trail: If you want to reach Gold Peak itself, continue past this spur road on Gold Peak Road for another mile, to the intersection with the North Fork of Gold Creek Road. Gold Peak Road continues as a somewhat overgrown track to the left. The road leads through a shady grove of red alder. After 0.3 miles, a landslide blocks the road.

STEAMPOT CREEK

A trail through deep forest on an old logging road that joins Toll Road and East Fork Road; it features many small stream crossings.

Difficulty	Trailhead Coordinates
Moderate	45.360711, -123.547824
Distance	Elevation
4.5 miles round-trip	1,065 feet gain

Suggested Maps
USGS Yamhill River topographic map

24

GETTING THERE

From Portland, drive west on US-26, then OR-6, toward Tillamook. About 3 miles before Tillamook (about a mile after the Wilson River Canyon opens up into the Wilson River flood plain), turn left at a sign for Trask River Road. This actually puts you on Olson Road for about 2 miles before reaching the actual sign for Trask River Road. At the Trask River Road sign, turn left just before a bridge over the Trask River. Follow this road to Trask County Park at milepost 12. To start the hike from East Fork Road, continue past the campground. Where the road turns to gravel past a one-lane bridge, continue for about 0.5 miles. Turn left on a road marked by a fish (which leads to a fish hatchery), and after 0.2 miles, turn right onto the unsigned East Fork Road, a well-maintained gravel road with spectacular views. Follow the road 5.1 miles to the trailhead just before a bridge over Steampot Creek and a marked junction with Camp Murphy Road Park at the trailhead.

To start the hike, follow the trail along Steampot Creek. At 0.25 miles, cross a side creek, taking care on the steep banks. Continue walking along the main creek through alder forest, past banks of sword ferns. At 0.75 miles, cross

Photo courtesy of Riley Pittenger

another creek where there are remnants of a road bridge. After a short distance, cross yet another creek and start a gradual climb. Continue to an open meadow at about 1.5 miles. At the far side, cross another creek. Where the trail appears to split, stay left and recross the same creek where it's spanned by a nurse log with sizable trees growing from it. Climb more steeply as firs replace alders. Cross a very small creek and continue on the trail until you meet the road at almost 2.25 miles. At this point you can climb 10 yards to the road and turn right, or continue a few hundred yards down and then up to reach the Toll Road junction.

For a scenic lunch spot, cross both roads at the junction and look for a trail that heads north on the opposite side. Follow the trail for a few hundred yards to a pond and wetland area. To return to the East Fork Road Trailhead, retrace your steps from the Toll Road junction.

JOYCE CREEK

25

Suggested
Maps
USGS
Trask, OR
Quadrangle

A beautiful walk along an old road to a picnic spot overlooking Bill Creek. Be sure to be on the lookout for elk, which are often found in the area.

Difficulty	Trailhead Coordinates
Moderate	45.387604, -123.616531
Distance	Elevation
About 7 miles round-trip, or about 5 miles round-trip if driving further in	1,165 feet gain

GETTING THERE

From Portland, drive west on US-26, then OR-6, toward Tillamook. Watch the mileposts indicating the remaining distance to Tillamook. About 3 miles before Tillamook (about a mile after the Wilson River Canyon opens up into the Wilson River flood plain), turn left at a sign for Trask River Road; this actually puts you on Olson Road first. Follow this road for about 2 miles and upon reaching the sign for Trask River Road, turn left just before a bridge over the Trask River. Follow Trask River Road past Trask County Park at milepost 12 and continue where it turns to gravel after crossing a one-lane bridge. Pass a side road marked by a fish sign that leads to a fish hatchery. Stay on the well-maintained main road (now South Fork Road) which follows the South Fork of the Trask River.

Photo courtesy of Riley Pittenger

Just past the 2.5-mile sign and before a bridge, look for a sandy, unmarked road (Joyce Creek Road) rising steeply to the right. If you have a vehicle with four-wheel drive, you can follow this road for almost a mile to a berm and deep ditch, taking care as you cross drainage ditches (this will shorten your hike by almost 2 miles round-trip). If you don't have four-wheel drive, park at the junction and start your walk here.

From the (unmarked) entrance to Joyce Creek Road, walk uphill for almost a mile. Continue through alder forest fringed with huge sword ferns, passing occasional meadows with expansive views of the Joyce Creek Valley. Joyce Creek is remarkably wide for a small creek.

Along the way, watch for signs of abundant elk—steep side trails and flattened vegetation in meadows—as well as wildflowers in meadows and on open hillsides. About 2.5 miles from the Joyce Creek Road turnoff, come to a level grove of alders and, at 3 miles, to another berm and the end of the road. Skirt the berm and push through some overhanging vegetation to find a trail that continues another 0.5 miles to an open area on the shoulder between Joyce Creek and Bill Creek—a great picnic spot with a view of Bill Creek.

From the picnic site, you can explore the open hillside overlooking Bill Creek. The hillside offers a view of Grindstone Mountain across the creek and ends in an elk meadow. Retrace your steps to return to your car.

Illustration courtesy of Lori LaBissoniere

MIAMI-KILCHIS DRAINAGE

CEDAR BUTTE

A short, steep hike to a gorgeous panoramic viewpoint overlooking the southern Tillamook Forest. May be combined with the Feldshaw Ridge hike, as both originate from the same trailhead.

Suggested Maps
Wild Salmon Center and Outdoor Project Wilson River Map

Difficulty	Trailhead Coordinates
Moderate	45.5829, -123.6473
Distance	Elevation
1.5 miles round-trip	707 feet gain

GETTING THERE

From Portland, drive west on US-26, then OR-6, toward Tillamook. From OR-6,

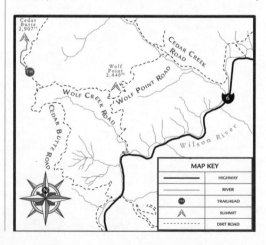

turn onto Cedar Butte Road just west of milepost 18. Proceed uphill on this well-maintained gravel road for 5.6 miles, avoiding several side roads and logging spurs along the way. Shortly before reaching the butte, there will be a parking area on the right where you can leave your car. Walk back across Cedar Butte Road and up an unmarked road leading west for about 100 yards to the well-marked Cedar Butte Trailhead.

Photo courtesy of Brian Pasko

The first half of the hike stays relatively level as you traverse through a clearcut roughly paralleling the road. Once you reach the foot of the butte, however, the character of the hike changes dramatically. You will ascend steeply, past nearly two dozen switchbacks through the mixed forest, until the trail finally breaks out into the clearing at the top of Cedar Butte. From here, take a moment to rest on the summit bench and enjoy the far-reaching views, then retrace your steps to return to your car.

FELDSHAW RIDGE

A short hike requiring basic orienteering skills on elk paths. Spectacular views of Cedar Butte and the Sawtooth Ridge. May be combined with the Cedar Butte hike, as both start from the same trailhead.

Suggested Maps
2012 Northwest Oregon Protection District Map

27

Difficulty
Easy to moderate; one short, very steep section

Trailhead Coordinates
45.5829, -123.6473

Distance
2.2 miles round-trip

Elevation
150 feet gain

GETTING THERE
From Portland, drive west on US-26, then OR-6, toward Tillamook. Once on OR-6, turn onto Cedar Butte Road just west of milepost 18. Proceed uphill on this well-maintained gravel road for 5.6 miles, avoiding several side roads and logging spurs along the way. Shortly before reaching the Butte, there will be a parking area on the right where you can leave your car. Walk back across Cedar Butte Road and up an unmarked road leading west for about 100 yards until you reach the well-marked Cedar Butte Trailhead.

For the Feldshaw Ridge hike, continue west on the road from the trailhead for another 200 yards to an intersection, where you will angle to the left. Pass through a broad, flat area in the road at 0.35 miles, disregarding several OHV trails which lead off to the right. Staying on the road, you will ascend a small rise, then descend again to a second broad, flat area at 0.7 miles. Looking straight ahead to the end of this stretch, you will see a very steep trail leading upwards into the woods, which gains 150 feet elevation in the next 0.1 miles.

At the top, continue straight as the trail (mercifully) levels out a bit. When you reach a fork in the path at the base of a hill, go to the right. Curve west around the base of two hilltops to a rudimentary campsite (no water), with limited views to the south. Beyond this point, the trail will fade to an elk path. Stay on the ridge for another 0.1 miles until you reach the rocky promontory at the west end of Feldshaw Ridge. Watch your footing at the top, as the north side is quite steep. Enjoy the unique vantage point of Cedar Butte and the magnificent Sawtooth Ridge, then retrace your steps back to the car. On the way down, take extra care on the steep section, which can be unexpectedly slippery in spots even if the ground is dry.

SAWTOOTH RIDGE

28

Suggested
Maps
USGS
Cedar Butte
Quadrangle
topographic
map

A hike along a rugged, trail-like road and around Sawtooth Ridge. Much of the hike is through a beautiful alder grove, and the trail can be difficult to follow in places. Requires a map and strong orienteering skills.

Difficulty	Trailhead Coordinates
Strenuous	45.622408, -123.74195

Distance	Elevation
8 miles round-trip	About 1,300 feet gain

GETTING THERE

From Portland, drive west on US-26, then OR-6, toward Tillamook. Turn north onto US-101 (the main coast highway) and at a sign for the Kilchis River, turn right onto Alderbrook Loop Road. At the first T-intersection, turn right toward Kilchis County Park. Follow Kilchis River Road for 1.3 miles, and you'll see a bridge to your right. Turn right and cross the bridge. You'll see a day use area to the left—your last chance to use a restroom. Continue along the south side of the river, avoiding side roads, for about 11 miles. Park in the gravel turnout just before the bridge across the North Fork of the Kilchis. Kilchis River

Photo courtesy of T. J. Carter

Road is navigable for passenger vehicles, but make sure you have strong tires for the sharp gravel.

Start walking up the occasionally steep four-wheel drive road to the right of Kilchis River Road—a road marked "Sawtooth Ridge Road." At about 0.5 miles, stay right at the fork, and then go left at the next fork. After another 0.25 miles, take a right at the next fork and walk up the steeper of the two roads. When you reach a saddle (a small dip in the land), the road becomes rough and trail-like. Head down the trail-like road and walk through the beautiful alder grove. You'll encounter trees that have blown down and areas of considerable erosion, creating steep sections.

After approximately 2 miles, the road flattens out into a backcountry campsite area.

From the flat area, follow the elk trail up the ridge, then turn right after about 100 yards. Follow the contour line along the ridge, staying more or less at the same elevation. Here is where the trail becomes difficult to follow. You should be fine as long as you keep the ridge on your left side. After about a mile, you'll come to the pointed end of the ridge. Walk around it and continue along the other side of the ridge for another 0.5 miles. Retrace your steps to get back to your car. All along the trail, you will likely see bobcat and elk scat. If you're lucky, you might see a few elk and deer as well. Sawtooth Ridge is an especially rewarding place to visit in late spring and early summer, when you'll find a profusion of subalpine wildflowers.

WEST END OF SAWTOOTH RIDGE

A sometimes-steep hike up a logging spur and elk trails to impressive views Mutt Peak and the South Fork Kilchis drainage. Requires orienteering skills and a map.

		Suggested Maps
Difficulty	Trailhead Coordinates	USGS
Moderate to strenuous	45.622408, -123.74195	Cedar Butte Quadrangle topographic map

Distance	Elevation
4.6 miles round-trip	1,485 feet gain

GETTING THERE

From Portland, drive west on US-26, then OR-6, toward Tillamook. Turn north onto US-101 (the main coast highway) and at a sign for the Kilchis River, turn right onto Alderbrook Loop Road. At the first T-intersection, turn right toward Kilchis County Park. Follow Kilchis River Road for 1.3 miles, and you'll see a bridge to your right. Turn right and cross the bridge. You'll see a day use area to the left—your last chance to use a restroom. Continue along the south side of the river, avoiding side roads, for about 11 miles. Park in the gravel turnout just before the bridge across the North Fork of the Kilchis. Kilchis River Road is navigable for passenger vehicles, but make sure you have strong tires for the sharp gravel.

Start walking up the occasionally steep four-wheel drive road to the right of Kilchis River Road—a road marked "Sawtooth Ridge Road." At about 0.5 miles, stay right at the fork, and then go left at the next fork. After another 0.25 miles, take a right at the next fork and walk up the steeper of the two roads. When you reach a flat gap at 1.5

Photo courtesy of T. J. Carter

miles, look for a faint upward path in front of a jumble of rocks to the east-northeast. Follow this path along the south-facing side of the rocks and ridge. As you hike, watch for coyote, elk, deer, and bobcat tracks and scat.

At 1.8 miles, the path veers left to the top of the ridge and becomes steep. Follow the ridge as far as possible using the elk trails on the south side of the ridge crest. From the open sections of the ridge, you'll have 360-degree views of the Tillamook Forest. A rocky knob followed by a brushy, difficult gap is a good place to stop. From this point you can see the impressive 2,241-foot Mutt Peak and the drainage of the wild South Fork of the Kilchis River. Retrace your steps to return to the trailhead.

Miami-Kilchis
Drainage

COMPANY CREEK

A hike through the deep woods of Company Creek canyon to a saddle with a view of the Little South Fork of the Kilchis River in its rugged, wild drainage. A short hike due to a major washout from heavy rains, but worthwhile if you're in the area.

Difficulty	Trailhead Coordinates
Moderate	45.6028, -123.7538

Distance	Elevation
2 miles round-trip	Up to 500 feet

GETTING THERE

From Portland, drive west on US-26 and then on OR-6 to Tillamook. At Highway 101, go north 3.7 miles and turn right at Idaville Road. Continue east on Alderbrook Road for 0.7 miles, bearing left at the bend onto Kilchis River Road. Drive another 1.3 miles and turn right to cross the bridge onto Kilchis River Forest Road. From here on, the road is hard gravel with lots of potholes. Keep left along this road to follow the Kilchis River for 9.1 miles, passing a few active logging roads. Take note of a very large tree stump next to the road 0.1 miles before Company Creek Road, which

Suggested Maps 2012 Northwest Oregon Protection District Map

30

is unmarked; in fact, it looks more like a leafy driveway rising to the right. Drive up Company Creek Road for 0.2 miles and park; the wide area is big enough for a car to turn around. Just beyond this, an earthen berm has been built across the road to limit access to foot traffic only.

Climb over the berm and start your hike. Nature is reclaiming this road, which is slowly disintegrating, rocky, and overgrown. The road is partially washed out half a mile beyond the start. Then, at about 1 mile, just beyond a large, fallen aspen, the road ends at a sharp drop-off from a washed-out section. Take a moment to gaze longingly at the road continuing on the other side before retracing your steps to return to your car.

While this route takes you high above the South Fork of the Kilchis River, picnicking and swimming are possible along the lower reaches of the river. When returning from the hike, turn right onto the main road. Take the next side road to the right, just past the South Fork of the Kilchis, and drive in a short way to a washout. Park here and walk to a dispersed camping area just up the road. This is a good spot for a picnic, and the stream has an amazingly clear, blue pool that's safe for swimming.

Kilchis River County Park and Campground features 40 tent campsites (fee required), fishing, a boat launch and a chance to see old-growth trees.

KILCHIS RIVER

This is a peaceful hike running along the Kilchis River. Heavily forested with access to the river in some spots. Starting out level, the trail slowly veers up from the river before turning abruptly and steeply following a ridge up to a small, seasonal waterfall.

Suggested Maps
Kilchis River Quadrangle topographic map

31

Difficulty
Moderate

Trailhead Coordinates
45.585824, -123.794622

Distance
4.8 miles
round-trip

Elevation
1,100 feet gain

GETTING THERE

From Portland, drive west on US-26, then OR-6 toward Tillamook, and turn north onto US-101 toward Bay City. About 2 miles north of Tillamook, turn right on Alderbrook Loop Road and follow the sign for Kilchis County Park. At the next T-intersection, turn right, still following signs to the park. Follow the river until you reach a sign reading "Kilchis County Park 3 miles." Turn right at the sign and cross a small bridge, continuing now on unpaved Kilchis River Road. This is a rough road, dusty in the summer. Follow the Kilchis

River for almost 7 miles, keeping to the left of any Y in the road. Take the first full left turn you reach, cross the bridge, and park in the pullout on the right side.

Scenic Kilchis River Road affords numerous views of the emerald green Kilchis River. The road passes giant maples and some of the largest Sitka spruce remaining in the Tillamook Forest. Just past Sam Downs Road, there's an especially nice picnic spot at a sandy beach down a lane that starts beside a 10-foot-wide Sitka spruce. A few lovely dispersed campsites dot the river as well.

Start your hike by walking onto the bridge and looking down at a pool 15- to 20-feet deep. On a bright summer day, you can see a long underwater canyon beneath the surface of the glassy yellow-green water. Scramble down the steep bank near your car to explore a huge table of rock along the river. Here, you'll find a deep pool (a great picnic spot when you return from your hike). The trail follows a level or gently rolling dirt road along the river to the right of the bridge.

There's usually very little, if any, traffic on this quiet, dead-end road—with the possible exception of hunting season. As you hike, you'll have glimpses of the lazy, sprawling Kilchis through stands of hemlock, spruce, and alder trees. At certain points, you can see the shallow gravel beds that make the Kilchis such an important spawning river for native fish.

Soon after starting the hike, you'll see a clearing with a Fish America Foundation sign on your right. This is

a small alder-conversion project where alders have been cleared and conifers planted in their place. ODF believes alders are not as useful to fish-bearing streams as conifers, which can grow larger and eventually fall into the river to create pools where fish can hide.

Photo courtesy of Chris Smith

After about a mile, watch for a lane veering right. For a short detour, follow the lane to a curve in the river with a gravel bar and huge moss-covered boulders. This also makes a good picnic spot. From the fork on the main road, start climbing, moving farther away from the river. After about 1.5 miles, the road starts to disintegrate, turning into a rutted, muddy gully. This brief steep section is passable in dry weather but would be very slippery in wet conditions.

Once you pass the eroded section, the road becomes more of a grassy lane or trail through the forest, continuing its ascent at a more moderate grade. At about 2 miles, you'll come to a rock outcropping that rises up to 200 feet above you on your right. To your left, you can catch glimpses of the Kilchis River valley through the trees. A seasonal creek with a tiny waterfall that crosses the trail marks the end of the hike. Retrace your steps to return to the trailhead.

LITTLE SOUTH FORK KILCHIS RIVER

A pleasant hike above the Little South Fork canyon with expansive views of the surrounding forested peaks.

Difficulty	Trailhead Coordinates
Moderate	45.556473, -123.754417

Distance	Elevation
6 miles round-trip	1,260 feet gain

Suggested Maps
USGS Cedar Butte Quadrangle topographic map

32

GETTING THERE

From Portland, drive west on US-26, then OR-6, toward Tillamook. Turn north onto US-101 toward Bay City. About 2 miles north of Tillamook, turn right on Alderbrook Loop Road, where you'll see a sign for the Kilchis River and Kilchis County Park. At the next T-intersection, turn right, still following signs to the park. Follow the Kilchis River until you reach a sign that says "Kilchis County Park 3 miles." Turn right at the sign and cross a small bridge, continuing now on unpaved Kilchis River Road (while four-wheel drive is unnecessary, good tires are recommended because of sharp rocks). Make sure to keep left at a fork. About 3 miles from the first bridge, turn right onto primitive, steeper Sam Downs Road, which is passable for sturdy passenger cars in most weather. Cross three small bridges. Just after the third bridge, about 2.3 miles from Kilchis River Road, turn left at a fork. Follow this even more primitive road past dispersed campsites on the Little South Fork and through a small clearcut where the road can be potholed and muddy. Park in a small pullout at the next fork, or alternatively, park at the campsites and walk the extra distance.

Start your hike on a small lane that forks right and passes through a grove of wild cherries, big-leaf maple, and alder, with the bubbling sounds of the Little South Fork below. At a fork in the lane, turn left, negotiating two trenches and continuing on what now becomes a rutted, sometimes muddy, moderately steep path. (The right fork leads to an informal campsite along the creek, clearly a favorite spot for bear and elk, judging from the ample scat under the trees.)

At the next fork in the trail, you'll see a large gully created by rainwater. Turn right onto a grassy lane that climbs steadily but moderately and opens to views of the surrounding forested peaks. Continue walking far above the Little South Fork canyon on a rolling lane (an elk and coyote highway) that ducks into the forest and out again for expansive views. Note the whitened snags—evidence of the Tillamook Burn—still towering over the younger forest.

In this section of the trail, you'll need to negotiate a

Photo courtesy of Chris Smith

few minor washouts. Watch for a clearcut on a steep hill to your right and note the resulting landslides. On your left, you'll pass rock outcroppings with interesting plant life. Even though you're less than 10 miles from the ocean, you're unlikely to encounter a soul on this peaceful hike.

At about 2 miles, come to a huge logjam that has totally blocked a tributary of the Little South Fork. Pick your way across the left side along a small, somewhat obscure footpath. At the far side of the logjam, veer right on the footpath (past a small waterfall) which will turn back into a grassy lane. Continue to a viewpoint where you can look back at the Little South Fork valley and ridges behind you.

In a short distance, you'll come to a fork in the trail. The right fork descends to the river—a nice picnic spot. The main trail continues left toward Company Creek where huge logs create small waterfalls in the creek. At about 3 miles, the trail crosses Company Creek but is totally washed out. This is a good turnaround point where you can picnic on big boulders and munch red huckleberries when they're in season. Retrace your steps to return to the trailhead.

Illustration courtesy of Lori LaBissoniere

SALMONBERRY-NEHALEM DRAINAGE

FOUR COUNTY POINT TRAIL

A short hike along North Fork Wolf Creek through a Douglas-fir and alder forest to the only place in Oregon where the corners of four counties (Washington, Tillamook, Clatsop, and Columbia) meet. The point is identified by a granite marker on the ground.

Difficulty	Trailhead Coordinates
Easy	45.7805, -123.3517
Distance	Elevation
1.6 miles	116 feet gain

GETTING THERE
From Portland, drive west on US-26 to a point just past milepost 35. Watch for a brown sign with a hiker symbol on the right side of the road. Park here on the widened shoulder.

A wooden sign identifying the Four County Point Trail marks the beginning of your hike. Upon entering the forest, you'll immediately be confronted with an unmarked trail junction. Turn left and, from above, briefly contour the North Fork of Wolf

Suggested Maps
ODF Tillamook State Forest Trail Guide: Four County Point and Steam Donkey Trails

33

Creek before descending to the Wolf Creek stream itself. Along the trail, you'll pass through a beautiful Douglas-fir forest that is accented with vine maple, Oregon grape, salal, sword fern, bracken fern, vanilla leaf, and duck's foot.

At 0.1 miles, you'll reach a junction. The right fork ends in several yards at Wolf Creek, which is a good place for kids to look for snails, crayfish, and small fish, and for adults to admire

Photo courtesy of Riley Pittenger

the view up and down the stream. The left fork eventually veers away from the creek and ends a little less than a mile from the trailhead at Four Corners—a spot where the Washington, Tillamook, Clatsop, and Columbia counties meet. It's a serene spot, and although you're not out of earshot of US-26, the lush coastal rainforest will make you feel like you're a world apart from the 21st century. From here, retrace your steps to your car.

Combine this short hike with a rest stop picnic on your way to or from the coast, or simply use it as a way to stretch your legs and see a bit more of the forest than you would from your car.

Salmonberry-Nehalem Drainage

STEAM DONKEY TRAILS

Hike these two looped short trails at least once when you are driving through the forest. This is a great opportunity to see a piece of forest that was left as it was when loggers vacated instead of the miles of second growth and clearcut slopes on most of the drive from Portland to the Tillamook and Clatsop State Forests.

Suggested
Maps
ODF
Tillamook
State Forest
Trail Guide:
Four County
Point and
Steam Donkey
Trails

Difficulty	Trailhead Coordinates
Easy	45.7963, -123.4589

Distance	Elevation
0.3 miles (Springboard Loop trail); 0.5 miles (Dooley Spur trail)	50 feet (Springboard Loop trail); 200 feet (Dooley Spur trail)

GETTING THERE

From US-26, drive into the Sunset Rest Area on the north side of the road between mileposts 28 and 29.

Read the story of the forest on the interpretive signs in the center of the rest area, then find the trailhead in the northwestern corner. Cross a bridge over Wolf Creek and come to the beginning of the Springboard loop. Take either direction on the short trail and come to a second junction and a sign explaining the operation of the steam donkey, a type of engine used for logging. Look at the huge remaining stumps and imagine how the forest looked to the loggers who stood on the springboards and sawed giant trees.

Continue on the second loop and climb steadily through a mass of fallen logs, stumps, and new trees. Watch for springboards, nurse logs, and stumps with new growth, sometimes with several new trees growing from them. Loop back down to the junction along an old railroad bed and back to the rest area; you will be able to glimpse Wolf Creek as you do so.

Photo courtesy of T. J. Carter

SALMONBERRY RIVER OVERVIEW

This guide includes four hikes along the Salmonberry River, the largest roadless river in the Tillamook Forest. From its origin near Timber, the Salmonberry flows west 19 miles to its confluence with the Nehalem River. The Salmonberry is home to one of the last healthy runs of wild steelhead in Oregon. The Association of Northwest Steelheaders and Native Fish Society volunteers have run a successful fish monitoring program to help understand and improve the river's winter steelhead habitat. The Salmonberry also provides habitat for cutthroat and rainbow trout, and in the fall, chinook and coho salmon.

The Salmonberry Canyon has produced its share of cautionary tales dating back to days of hugely difficult and dangerous timber extraction. The modern hiker should be aware that the terrain and torrential downpours of the Coast Range have left portions of the Port of Tillamook Bay Railroad tracks unstable or destroyed. Questions about the future of the tracks and the right-of-way remain unanswered. Access is unauthorized.

To hike the Salmonberry, begin at the Nehalem River, Beaver Slide Road, or Cochran Trailhead and simply follow the railroad tracks upriver or downriver as far as you want to go. Along much of the route, you must walk on the railroad tracks, which some people find tiring. The ties probably won't fit your stride, and you may not like walking on the rock ballast. Some people also dislike the odor of creosote. However, certain sections of the route have stretches of trail beside the tracks that make for easier walking.

The railroad also has numerous tunnels and trestles. The tunnels range in length from about 50 feet to 150 feet. While it's helpful to bring a flashlight with you (especially for the longer tunnels), it's not absolutely necessary. The trestles are specially fitted with aluminum grates for hiker safety. In some places, you can view the river from a trestle directly above the rushing water.

Along the scenic and remote Salmonberry, you can see an abundance of native flora and fauna, such as water ouzels diving for insects. There are many spots to enjoy the scenery, go fishing, hop in for a swim, bask on a boulder or log, or have a picnic. Taking it slow and stopping often makes exploring the river a fun and unusual outing.

The railroad was built in 1911 and helped evacuate people during the Tillamook Burn. The mileposts along the tracks are actually distances from San Francisco. In 2007, a storm coupled with inadequate logging rules led to numerous landslides in the canyon, wiping out the railroad at several points. Remnant tracks are violently bent into the river at points, and railroad ties and other equipment can be found scattered throughout the canyon. It is a phenomenal example of nature—the amazing combination of water, wind, and steep slopes of the Oregon Coast Range—refusing to be tamed.

There is currently a proposal to create the Salmonberry Trail which would convert the old rail line into a multi-use trail connecting the Banks-Vernonia bike path to the Coast. The project could be a huge draw for Oregonians who love

Salmonberry-
Nehalem Drainage

the outdoors, especially the rapidly growing population of Washington County. Questions remain about local input, crowding, sanitation, and how a developed trail would affect this sensitive ecosystem.

Photo courtesy of Josh Kulla

PENNOYER CREEK AND SALMONBERRY RIVER

A moderate hike alongside old railroad tracks. The trail is well-maintained with little elevation change; however, tunnels and trestles make it unsuitable for children or those with a fear of heights. Be sure to bring a flashlight.

Difficulty	Trailhead Coordinates
Easy to moderate	45.704539, -123.411053

Distance	Elevation
9 miles round-trip	Little change

Suggested Maps
Outdoor Project: Upper Salmonberry River

SALMONBERRY CLOSURES

As of press time, the hikes along the historic Salmonberry Railroad are closed to public access due to unsafe conditions. This includes Pennoyer Creek and Salmonberry River, North Fork of the Salmonberry to Enright, North Fork of the Salmonberry to Wolf Creek Flats, Lower Salmonberry Trail, and any others making use of the railroad right-of-way. These hike descriptions are included for information only until hazardous conditions have been resolved. Ooligan Press, the Sierra Club, and contributing writers assume no responsibility for accidents, injuries, or other incidents resulting from misuse of trail information.

Please note that the Salmonberry River Corridor is currently the focus of a comprehensive plan to create an extensive trail system across western Oregon. For more information and opportunities to get involved, please visit *salmonberrytrail.org.*

ALWAYS CHECK FOR CURRENT TRAIL CLOSURES
on the Oregon Department of Forestry website.

GETTING THERE
Take US-26 west out of Portland until you hit Timber Road. Take a left (south) down Timber Road just after milepost 38. Continue 3 miles to the town of Timber before making a right onto Cochran Road. This road is fairly well-maintained but does get a bit bumpy in places. Follow the road until you hit a three-way split. Take the left fork and you should come across railroad tracks. Park here and go to the right. After hiking a little alongside the tracks, you should come to Cochran Pond. If you don't see the pond, you're going the wrong way and should turn around.

The entire hike is alongside tracks that are no longer in use. If you're feeling adventurous, you can follow the tracks for quite a while. The path is mainly flat. During the first mile of the hike, you may hear gunshots. Don't be alarmed: the shots are from a shooting area far above the tracks.

There are some places along the hike where the tracks span chasms. Several of these chasms have metal grating covering the ties, but not all of them. For those that don't, step carefully across the railroad ties.

Make sure the area is safe to cross. At the time that this book was written, the ties are sound, but they might not be in the future.

Just before the end of the second mile, you'll reach a tunnel. The tunnel is not long, but does get dark in the middle, so a flashlight is advisable. Be cautious—the stability of tunnels can change over time. The trail merges with the tracks beyond the tunnel, so you'll need to walk mostly along the tracks.

Between the second and third miles, you'll cross the incredible Big Baldwin trestle on a walkway beside the tracks. It's about 150 feet long and sits high above the ground in the Salmonberry River canyon. It's a nice place to stop for a snack; just be mindful of tar, as it can stick to skin and clothing and is hard to get off.

If you walk along the tracks for another 1 to 2 miles, you'll pass through a little meadow before coming to a second, shorter tunnel. On the other side of this tunnel is a smaller trestle; this is the Little Baldwin Creek trestle. At this point, the trail becomes more overgrown; going further requires some bushwhacking, which makes this a good stopping point. From here, retrace your route to the start of the hike.

NORTH FORK OF THE SALMONBERRY TO ENRIGHT

Suggested
Maps
USGS
Cochran and
Rogers Peak
Quadrangles
topographic
maps

A scenic, secluded walk following the North Fork and main Salmonberry rivers, offering a chance to see a deserted rail town and to see steelhead jumping up a waterfall in spring. It is recommended that you bring a flashlight for tunnels and sandals or sneakers for stream crossing. To check on current accessibility, call the Port of Tillamook Bay at 503-842-2413.

Difficulty	Trailhead Coordinates
Moderate to strenuous	45.75001, -123.65223

Distance	Elevation
10.3 miles round-trip	1,745 feet gain

SALMONBERRY CLOSURES

As of press time, the hikes along the historic Salmonberry Railroad are closed to public access due to unsafe conditions. This includes Pennoyer Creek and Salmonberry River, North Fork of the Salmonberry to

Enright, North Fork of the Salmonberry to Wolf Creek Flats, Lower Salmonberry Trail, and any others making use of the railroad right-of-way. These hike descriptions are included for information only until hazardous conditions have been resolved. Ooligan Press, the Sierra Club, and contributing writers assume no responsibility for accidents, injuries, or other incidents resulting from misuse of trail information.

Please note that the Salmonberry River Corridor is currently the focus of a comprehensive plan to create an extensive trail system across western Oregon. For more information and opportunities to get involved, please visit *salmonberrytrail.org*.

ALWAYS CHECK FOR CURRENT TRAIL CLOSURES
on the Oregon Department of Forestry website.

GETTING THERE
From Portland, drive west on US-26 toward Seaside. Just past milepost 32, turn left onto Salmonberry Road. This gravel road requires a high-clearance vehicle, and depending on the weather, four-wheel drive may be necessary for the last section. (Do not attempt to drive on the road in snow.) It will take you close to an hour to drive the next 12 miles to the trailhead. Continue heading southwest on Salmonberry Road; pass Section 10 and Camp 5, as well as the Rock Creek, Wheeler, Shields, and Cochran roads. (Make sure to carry and use a map, as it is easy to become confused and take a wrong turn.) At the intersection of

Salmonberry-Nehalem Drainage

Salmonberry Road and Cochran Road, be sure to stay on Salmonberry Road by taking the middle fork. Do not take the right fork that heads west—this is a very bad section of Salmonberry Road that loops back from the trailhead. At 9 miles, you'll reach Camp 9; continue straight on what is now North Fork Road. Proceed carefully on the narrow, steep, curvy, and rocky road, using four-wheel drive if conditions are wet. After about 3 miles, come to the North Fork of the Salmonberry and park at a landing before the road is blocked.

Walk down a grassy, alder-lined lane high above the North Fork of the Salmonberry on your right. The grade seems easy on the descent but can be tiring to hike back up at the end of the day. You may have to skirt old rock slides early in the hike. Notice how vegetation has started to reclaim this recently closed road; in spring, it fills with wildflowers such as bleeding heart and monkey flower. On one side, the road is bordered by a mossy cliff where rainwater drips over maidenhair ferns and fringecup flowers.

When the leaves are off the alders, you can see waterfalls tumbling through the narrow basalt chasm beneath you. Look for the biggest of these waterfalls at about 1.5 miles. If you're nimble and a bit daring, you can scramble down the steep, obstacle-strewn embankment to get a closer look at the falls. This route is sometimes marked with an orange ribbon. In the spring, your effort might be rewarded with the sight of winter steelhead leaping up the boiling waterfall, almost clearing the top, then crashing back into

Photo courtesy of Chris Smith

the swirling cauldron to try again. You may find yourself compelled to root for the steelhead, awestruck by their resilience and tenacity against the formidable challenges they face.

If you can pull yourself away from the steelhead, continue on the trail to a clearing (now an informal campsite above the Salmonberry) and turn right onto a path to the confluence of the North Fork and Salmonberry at about 2 miles. Scramble down a steep, muddy embankment to the main stream, then pick your way across a gravel bar to the left of a cable that spans the river. To continue the hike, ford the river in this wide, knee-deep shallow stretch. Bring extra shoes, as the water is too cold to cross barefoot.

(Do not attempt the crossing unless the water level is low.) Scramble up the opposite bank on one of the eroded paths about 50 yards west of the old railroad tie on the bank. At the top, come to a grassy area where old railroad tracks have been overgrown. Follow the railroad grade to the right as it curves down the hill and, in about 500 yards, meets the river and a railroad tunnel on your left.

Turn right on the rail line to continue your hike along the Salmonberry. To check on current accessibility, call the Port of Tillamook Bay at 503-842-2413. Walk on or beside the tracks for the next 3 miles to the abandoned town of Enright. Where the track curves left, you'll see signs of a landslide with an eroded, bowl-shaped area to the left of the tracks and a silt fence attempting to protect the river. Parts of the railroad collapse into the river now and then, sometimes smothering spawning beds.

Beyond a culvert, pass through a short railroad tunnel. Look and listen for trains (which you can hear miles away) or automobiles on adapter wheels before entering the tunnel. After the tunnel, the canyon is especially attractive, with basalt rocks descending to clear pools and riffles.

Because you are right above the river, it's easy to spot steelhead trout redds, or nests. Look for flat, gravelly circles that appear whiter than the rest of the moss-covered rocks. This is where the fish have turned over the rocks to cover their eggs.

At about a mile from the confluence (before and after milepost 809), you'll need to cross two small trestle bridges. Walk on the grates provided by the Port of Tillamook Bay.

If they have fallen off, tread carefully over the slots in the bridge; be sure to watch for vehicles before you cross. Farther on, pass an old boxcar and go through a second tunnel before milepost 810, then a third tunnel a short distance after milepost 810. The river curves to the right here. You'll see a cable over the river and more signs of landslides.

After passing a railroad switch numbered 1638, you'll arrive at Enright (before milepost 811), marked by a small sign to the left of the tracks. In a cedar grove just beyond the sign is a small cabin. A few more buildings and a boxcar on tracks make up the remnants of the town. This is a fine place to picnic and dip your toes in the cold water before you retrace your steps to the trailhead.

The Enright and Belding logging camps were active during the early 1930s. Back then, a crew of 200 logged out of these camps. Logging was done by hand using two-man saws called "misery whips." Horses dragged the logs to the railroad. After the old growth had been selectively cut, the camps were essentially destroyed. However, the cabin still standing at Enright is the former office for the camps, now used as a private cabin.

Salmonberry-
Nehalem Drainage

NORTH FORK OF THE SALMONBERRY TO WOLF CREEK FLATS

A scenic and varied hike along the North Fork and main Salmonberry rivers offering challenges such as stream and trestle crossings and three tunnel passages. Flashlight recommended for tunnels; carry sandals or sneakers for stream crossing.

Suggested
Maps
USGS
Cochran and
Rogers Peak
Quadrangles
topographic
maps

Difficulty	Trailhead Coordinates
Moderate to strenuous	45.72835, -123.5062
Distance	Elevation
10.25 miles round-trip	2,470 feet gain

37

SALMONBERRY CLOSURES

As of press time, the hikes along the historic Salmonberry Railroad are closed to public access due to unsafe conditions. This includes Pennoyer Creek and Salmonberry River, North Fork of the Salmonberry to Enright, North Fork of the Salmonberry to Wolf Creek Flats, Lower Salmonberry Trail, and any others making use of the railroad right-of-way. These hike descriptions are included for information only until hazardous conditions have been resolved. Ooligan Press, the Sierra Club, and contributing writers assume no responsibility for accidents, injuries, or other incidents resulting from misuse of trail information.

Please note that the Salmonberry River Corridor is currently the focus of a comprehensive plan to create an extensive trail system across western Oregon. For more information and opportunities to get involved, please visit *salmonberrytrail.org.*

ALWAYS CHECK FOR CURRENT TRAIL CLOSURES
on the Oregon Department of Forestry website.

GETTING THERE
From Portland, drive west on US-26 toward Seaside. Just past milepost 32, turn left onto Salmonberry Road. This gravel road requires a high-clearance vehicle, and depending on the weather, four-wheel drive may be necessary for the last section. (Do not attempt to drive on the road in snow.) It will take you close to an hour to drive the next 12 miles to the trailhead. Continue heading southwest on Salmonberry Road; pass Section 10 and Camp 5, as well as the Rock Creek, Wheeler, Shields, and Cochran Roads. At the intersection of Salmonberry Road and Cochran Road, be sure to stay on Salmonberry Road by taking the middle fork. Do not take the right fork that heads west—this is a very bad section of Salmonberry Road that loops back from the trailhead. At 9 miles, you'll reach Camp 9; continue

straight on what is now North Fork Road. Proceed carefully on the narrow, steep, curvy, and rocky road, using four-wheel drive if conditions are wet. After about 3 miles, come to the North Fork of the Salmonberry and park at a landing before a dirt pile that blocks the road.

Walk down a grassy, alder-lined lane high above the North Fork of the Salmonberry on your right. The grade seems easy on the descent but can be tiring to hike back up at the end of the day. Follow this lovely lane for 2 miles along the cascading North Fork to its confluence with the main Salmonberry River. (See the North Fork Salmonberry to Enright hike description for information on where to look for steelhead jumping falls in the river.)

At the confluence, ford the stream, scramble up the opposite bank, and follow the old, overgrown railroad tracks to the left (the tracks on the right lead to Enright). When you come to the main railroad tracks to the left of a tunnel, follow these tracks away from the tunnel and along the river. From March through May, look for winter steelhead trout in the river; in the fall, watch for fall chinook salmon.

After milepost 807, less than a mile from the confluence, cross a series of small trestle bridges where the Salmonberry meanders sometimes to the right and sometimes to the left. If there are metal grates for walking, use them; otherwise, watch your step on as you cross the railroad ties. At a sharp bend in the river, pass through a drippy tunnel approximately 150 yards long. Be sure to carry a flashlight or headlamp for the briefly dark section

in the middle of the tunnel. Also make sure to listen and watch for slow-moving trains or faster, more dangerous rail-adapted trucks that may come down the tracks.

Beyond the tunnel, cross a steel bridge built in 1925 by walking on the pedestrian grates alongside the rails. Be careful—some of these walkways are not maintained. If you find loose sections, you may need to walk on the ties instead. Just before milepost 806—which is about 2 miles from the confluence—you'll come to Belding Crossing, where you'll see a hiker registration board provided by the Port of Tillamook Bay. If there are sign-in forms, you can sign in here, but there often are none. To the right is Beaver Slide Road, appropriately named for its steep descent from Salmonberry Road.

Salmonberry-
Nehalem Drainage

Soon you'll come to another tunnel about 175 yards long. Again, make sure to listen and watch for rail traffic and use a flashlight or headlamp in the dark section of the tunnel. Just beyond this tunnel is an especially nice place to picnic, either in the grassy area above the river or on the flat rocks in the river. Take time to enjoy this scenic spot with banks of ferns and mossy rocks lining the shore, creating a small chasm the river flows through.

Within the next mile, cross four small bridges over the meandering Salmonberry. Then enter another tunnel about 130 yards long, again taking care, and come out at Wolf Creek Flats, an area just before Wolf Creek where the Salmonberry flattens out in a wider valley. Pass a Southern Pacific metal shed and reach a grassy bench farther above the river. At one point, it looks as if the river jumped its banks and changed course. Follow the path away from the river to meet Wolf Creek.

A good turnaround point is a bit past milepost 805 where a red rock cliff has collapsed into Wolf Creek in a narrow, steep part of the canyon. It looks as if a concrete slab on the opposite side of the river fell with such force that it caused the cliff to collapse and completely block a prime fish spawning habitat. From this point, retrace your route to return to the trailhead.

LOWER SALMONBERRY TRAIL

A beautiful walk along the Lower Salmonberry from its confluence with the Nehalem River. It follows the railroad tracks to the current end of the tracks at about 3 miles. Although most of the time you will be walking along the ties between the rails, there is enough buildup of gravel to make it almost like walking on a level trail.

Suggested
Maps
2012
Northwest
Oregon
Protection
District Map

Difficulty	Trailhead Coordinates
Easy	45.75001, -123.65223

Distance	Elevation
6 miles round-trip	Almost no change

SALMONBERRY CLOSURES

As of press time, the hikes along the historic Salmonberry Railroad are closed to public access due to unsafe conditions. This includes Pennoyer Creek and Salmonberry River, North Fork of the Salmonberry to Enright, North Fork of the Salmonberry to Wolf Creek Flats, Lower Salmonberry Trail, and any others making use of the railroad right-of-way. These hike descriptions are included for information only until hazardous conditions have been resolved. Ooligan

38

Press, the Sierra Club, and contributing writers assume no responsibility for accidents, injuries, or other incidents resulting from misuse of trail information.

Please note that the Salmonberry River Corridor is currently the focus of a comprehensive plan to create an extensive trail system across western Oregon. For more information and opportunities to get involved, please visit *salmonberrytrail.org*.

ALWAYS CHECK FOR CURRENT TRAIL CLOSURES on the Oregon Department of Forestry website.

GETTING THERE

From Portland, drive west on US-26 to milepost 20. Turn left at a sign for Nehalem River Road. Drive about 12 miles on mostly paved road to the confluence of the Nehalem River and the Salmonberry River. There is a small parking area just before the railroad tracks and a bridge over the Salmonberry. The drive follows a beautiful stretch of the Nehalem through mostly alder forest and past a campground at Henry Rierson Spruce Run Campground. Just across the bridge over the Salmonberry, you will see the beautifully manicured grounds of Sunset Hunting Lodge, which boasts "no entry" signs.

Start up the railroad. At times, you will be hiking alongside the rails, but more frequently in the space between them. At first, the river will be on your right, but you will cross the river at least twice and will have many gorgeous views of deep eddies and lichen-covered rocks. If you are in the fall, you can also catch glimpses of fish on their journey upstream. The railroad is overgrown with vegetation and the forest rises steeply on

Photo courtesy of Rick Stare

both sides; watch and listen for kingfishers and dippers on the river. After about 2 miles, there is a point where a past landslide caused the railroad rails to hang out over the river, but it is easy to walk alongside on the trail.

At about 3 miles, the railroad comes to an abrupt end and the trail goes up into the forest. This is a good turning point and an opportunity to have lunch under a grove of lichen-covered alder trees. The trail continues for about another 5 level miles to Enright.

Return the way you came. The river looks even better in this direction.

There are plans to repair the railroad, and in the longer term, there is an ambitious multi-agency partnership to make this section part of a bike/pedestrian trail all the way from Wheeler on the coast to the Portland area.

Salmonberry-
Nehalem Drainage

STEP CREEK

A pleasant, gently rolling trail along Step Creek near the headwaters of the Nehalem River with an optional, longer return loop or a hike extension.

Suggested
Maps
USGS
Cochran
Quadrangle
topographic
map

Difficulty	Trailhead Coordinates
Moderate	45.70696, -123.33793
Distance	Elevation
2 miles round-trip	400 feet gain

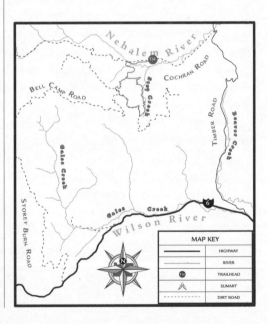

GETTING THERE

From Portland, drive west on US-26. After milepost 38, turn left onto Timber Road. Just before the railroad tracks, turn right onto Cochran Road, which turns into a gravel road after about 0.5 miles. Continue 2.3 miles to the ODF sign for Reehers Camp. You can also get to Cochran Road from the south via OR-6. Between mileposts 39 and 38, turn right (north) onto Timber Road. Continue 6.5 miles to Cochran Road and turn left. Drive just past Reehers Camp and the horse park to the day use area.

Walk to the large bulletin board that has an overview of the trails in the area. Begin your hike there. You'll see a sign indicating Gales Creek Trail that heads downhill toward the Nehalem River. The sign says 3.4 miles to Bell Camp. Stay on the trail and hike down to the river. The trail takes you back up to Cochran Road. Go 100 feet, cross the bridge, and turn left onto the trail again. A clearcut is on the right. In less than a quarter mile, cross the wooden foot bridge and stay on the trail as it works its way uphill across the railroad track. Just after you cross Round Top Road, veer left onto Step Creek Trail. To the right the Gales Creek Trail continues to Bell Camp.

Notice the carpet of sorrel and piggyback plants along the trail. Ferns (sword, bracken, spiny wood, and oak) also grow here in abundance. Trees include hemlock, cedar, Douglas-fir, alder, and vine maple. Other native plants you're likely to see are red elderberry, salmonberry, trillium, foam flower, self-heal, devil's club, and Oregon grape.

Salmonberry-
Nehalem Drainage

Photo courtesy of Brian Pasko

As the trail curves uphill to Rice Road, look for an overgrown road to the left that continues about 100 feet to an
open wetland created by a beaver dam on the creek. After
exploring the wetland, backtrack to the main trail and continue to Rice Road. From here, return the way you came
or extend your hike through one or both of the following
options.

To make a loop back to Reehers Camp, turn right onto
Rice Road. The loop will add about 3.5 miles to your trip
for a total of 5.5 miles. Follow Rice Road for about 0.75
miles, then turn right onto Round Top Road. Cross railroad tracks after about a mile on Round Top Road, then

reach Cochran Road within another 0.5 miles. Turn right onto Cochran Road and continue approximately 2 more miles to Reehers Camp.

You can extend your hike from Rice Road by turning left and following the road for 0.7 miles to Coffee Creek Road. This road is blocked to motorized traffic, but hikers and mountain bikers can follow it to see the other side of the valley. As you hike in this area, watch for coyote, deer and elk droppings and tracks. See if you can spot hawks in clearings. Replanted trees in the area are 10 to 20 years old. Older sections of the forest are marked for cutting in the near future.

Mountain bikers might be interested in an off-highway vehicle (OHV) trail just 0.1 miles past Coffee Creek Road on the left. The rutted trail offers steep, exhilarating ups and downs in short spurts. From a number of viewpoints, you can see the valley and surrounding mountains. The trail joins Rice Road periodically, then jets back up into the hills. It eventually ends at Dober Road. Although this area is currently closed to OHVs, their presence is evident.

If you extend your trip via one or both of the above options, retrace your route to the intersection of Rice Road and the trail from Reehers Camp. From here, you can return via the trail or take the longer loop back.

GIVEOUT MOUNTAIN SCENIC DRIVE

Suggested
Maps
USGS
Cochran
Quadrangle
topographic
map;
ODF 2002
Tillamook
State Forest
Visitor Map

This is not a hike but a scenic loop drive on well-maintained logging roads suitable for passenger cars to good views of Mount Jefferson, Mount Hood, Mount Adams, and Mount St. Helens.

Difficulty	Trailhead Coordinates
Moderate drive	45.707105, -123.341595

Distance	Elevation
20 miles round-trip	N/A

GETTING THERE

From Portland, drive west on US-26 and turn left (south) onto Timber Road between mileposts 38 and 37. Drive about 3 miles to the town of Timber. Just past the town center and before crossing the railroad tracks, turn right onto Cochran Road, which starts as paved and becomes a good gravel road suitable for sturdy passenger cars. After about 2 miles, just past Reehers Camp on the left, turn right on Wheeler Road. Continue uphill on this well-maintained gravel road for almost 3.2 miles, avoiding any side roads, until you reach two small fire protection roads on your left that are

40

Photo courtesy of Riley Pittenger

lined up immediately after each other. Turn left on the second of these roads, called Fire Protection Road #2.

As you drive uphill, you will see through mostly clearcut land to the left (southwest) and mostly second growth forest on the right. At about 2.3 miles, you will reach a plateau ridge called Giveout Mountain, perhaps because the slopes are known to slide easily; they do look as if they have slumped in the past. Weather permitting, the clearcuts afford impressive views of the Cascades—look for the sharp peak of Mount Jefferson in the distance to the south, and Mount Hood to the east. As you continue driving uphill, watch for the rounded summit of Mount Adams and flat-topped Mount St. Helens. At one especially spectacular viewpoint, you can see St. Helens, Adams, and Hood lined up in a perfect row, seeming very close together. On a winter day, you might see black clouds hovering over the dark ridges of the Tillamook Forest while the sun glistens on the snowy Cascade peaks.

After 3 miles, you will reach a left-hand turn to a spur road that leads you a few hundred feet to a log landing area with good views of Mount Jefferson to the south.

To continue your loop drive, return to Fire Protection Road #2, turn left, and proceed downhill through more clearcuts. You will pass a road on the right that is the continuation of Fire Protection Road #2. Go straight instead on what becomes Giveout Grade Road. At the next intersection, turn left to continue on Giveout Grade Road, where you enter forested land. Descend on this well-maintained road and be sure to avoid any side roads. In a large clearcut area, come to a T-intersection with Cochran Road. Turn left on Cochran Road to return to Reehers Camp and the town of Timber to complete the loop.

UPPER LOST CREEK RIDGE

With a steady but manageable incline, this trail peaks perfectly at the halfway point and has spectacular views of wildlife and the adjacent canyon.

Difficulty	Trailhead Coordinates
Easy to Moderate	45.711152, -123.633275

Distance	Elevation
4 miles round-trip	715 feet gain

Suggested Maps
2012 Northwest Oregon Protection District Map

GETTING THERE

From Portland, drive west on US-26 and turn left (south) onto Joe Woodard Road between mileposts 21 and 20 (you'll see a sign for Lower Nehalem River and Henry Rierson Spruce Run County Park). At a stop sign after 0.4 miles, turn left onto Lower Nehalem River Road. This scenic road starts out paved but eventually turns to gravel. Keep driving until you cross a bridge. Turn left on Tin Shack Road, which is between mileposts 9 and 10. Don't turn onto any logging spurs, especially the Lost Creek Ridge spur that veers right at about 3 miles from the turnoff for Tin Shack Road. At 4 miles from the turnoff, you'll come to a curve in the road. The road will curve slightly to the left and there will be two turnoffs to the

41

Photo courtesy of Brian Pasko

right; you can park in the lower one and start your hike on the upper one.

This grassy path is actually a logging spur called Upper Lost Creek Ridge Road. The straightforward road includes a few inclines and declines; it is mostly forested, but there are some breaks in the trees that allow for impressive views of the Tillamook State Forest.

Tracks and scat make it obvious that the route is an elk, deer, coyote, and grouse highway. The best views of the canyon and the forested ridges beyond are at almost 2 miles, where you can sit on a grassy bluff and eat your lunch. You can turn around here or continue along the road if you so wish.

NEHALEM FALLS LOOP

This short but beautiful loop around Nehalem Falls Campground includes views of the Nehalem River and Falls. The path also passes around a grove of old-growth spruce and cedar.

Difficulty   Trailhead Coordinates
Easy   45.72649, -123.77129

Distance   Elevation
0.7 miles   Approximately 100 feet gain

Suggested
Maps
Tillamook
State Forest
Recreation
Guide

GETTING THERE

There are two alternative routes from Portland. For the quicker route, turn south (left) from US-26 at milepost 21 on Lower Nehalem River Road (signposted to Henry Rierson Spruce Run Campground). You will drive a total of about 18 miles, some of which will be on gravel roads with potholes. The road is signposted again for Spruce Run Campground about 5 miles up the road. From the campground, you will be following the Nehalem River. The Nehalem Falls Campground is at milepost 7.

For a less picturesque and somewhat longer drive on paved roads, continue west on US-26. Turn south on OR-53 and follow

42

it toward US-101. About a mile before reaching US-101, turn south on Miami Foley Road, and after another mile turn left at a junction with Foss Road. Follow the Nehalem upstream to milepost 7.

Regardless of which route you choose, if the campground is closed, the entrance may not be obvious. Look for a yellow gate on a side road to the river at milepost 7.

Enter the campground and look for a sign between the two yellow gates for the Nehalem Falls Day Use Area. Walk down a short trail and admire the falls—they aren't readily distinguishable from the rest of the rapids when the river is running fast—and then find the trail upstream along the river. If you time this right—at the beginning of April—you will find the trail lined with a profusion of early blooming flowers, including a line of beautiful fawn lilies.

Follow the trail past the campground and along the edge of a rare grove of old-growth spruce and cedar. After about a half-mile loop uphill, you will return along the

upper edge of the campground to where you started. Take notice of the huge old stumps crowned with new young trees in the center of the campground.

Photo courtesy of Kristin Roosmalen

SOAPSTONE LAKE

This short, beautiful hike to a small forest lake in the drainage of the Nehalem River's North Fork offers close encounters with mature cedar and Sitka spruce trees; a good family hike for older children.

Suggested Maps
ODF Clatsop State Forest Recreation Guide

Difficulty	Trailhead Coordinates
Easy	45.84684, -123.76236

Distance	Elevation
2.2 miles round-trip	480 feet gain

GETTING THERE

From Portland, drive west on US-26 about 65 miles to the Necanicum junction. Turn left (south) onto OR-53 (Necanicum Highway) and continue 4.7 miles to where a marked gravel road joins the highway on the left. Turn onto this road, cross a bridge, and drive another 0.4 miles to a parking area on the left.

The trailhead is clearly marked leading up to the right from the parking area. Follow the trail through woods, over small bridges, and up wooden stairs made of railroad ties. A wooden bridge crosses Soapstone

43

Photo courtesy of Riley Pittenger

Creek. Continue uphill. After another 0.5 miles or so, you'll reach a T-intersection. This is where the trail becomes a loop. To the left you will continue over another bridge and quickly reach the lake. To the right you will shortly reach a fork in the trail marked by an ODF sign. Take that fork uphill to the left and walk around the lake. Whichever way you take from the T-intersection, you can cross the far end of the lake on a long, low bridge over the shallows.

At the north and south ends of the dark lake, you'll see large trees felled by beavers. As you explore the lakeshore, you'll encounter brushy and marshy areas as well as many fallen logs. Watch for salamanders and beaver.

NORTH FORK NEHALEM RIVER

A nearly level hike along a closed road on private timber company land featuring scenic views of the North Fork Nehalem River. The road may be closed during times of high fire danger and is posted as an active logging and hauling area.

Difficulty	Trailhead Coordinates
Easy	45.864609, -123.765256
Distance	Elevation
6.4 miles round-trip	250 feet gain

Suggested Maps
ODF Clatsop State Forest Recreation Guide

44

GETTING THERE

From Portland, drive west on US-26 to Necanicum Junction. Turn left (south) onto OR-53. Between mileposts 7 and 8, just before the fish hatchery, turn left onto unmarked Cole Mountain Road. At the immediate fork, bear right for a short distance and park at the pullout before the gate. The land beyond the gate is owned by a private timber company that permits walking on the road unless otherwise posted.

Start the hike on the road along the left side of the North Fork Nehalem River. Ignore the unsightly clearcut you'll pass on your left and instead keep your eyes on the very attractive alder- and Douglas-fir-lined river on your right. While you'll never be far from clearcut hillsides on this walk, the timber company has done a good job of leaving buffers along the river and much of the road, allowing hikers to feel as though they are walking through relatively undisturbed country.

At 0.9 miles, you'll cross a bridge with a swimming hole underneath it. Immediately after the bridge, veer left at a fork in the road and continue your walk, now on the right side of the river.

At 1.07 miles, you'll pass a series of pretty cascades, and at 1.4 miles, you'll reach a 15-foot waterfall near a fish ladder and a fish survey catch-and-release pen. After about 1.9 miles, the river, which is prime habitat for chinook salmon, steelhead trout, and cutthroat trout, becomes shallow, wide, and slow-moving. As you hike, watch for signs of great blue herons, black-tailed deer, and coyotes, and keep your eyes peeled for magnificent old-growth Sitka spruce and western hemlock.

Continue to follow the river, avoiding side roads that head uphill, and pass through a mixed forest of hemlock, Douglas-fir, spruce, cedar, alder, and big-leaf maple. On rocky ledges overlooking the river, you'll see "gardens" made up of a number of fern species. At 2.7 miles, where you'll encounter a bridge over a side creek, the road turns away from the river and soon passes a private hunting camp with picnic tables. It then goes through a highly disturbed area profuse with alder and at 3.2 miles crosses a bridge over the river where it enters state land.

At this point, you can continue to follow the road for another 6 miles if you like, but be aware that both passenger cars and RVs use it to access campsites and encountering logging trucks is always a possibility. Perhaps a better idea is to lounge on some of the excellent sunbathing rocks beneath the bridge before retracing your steps to your car.

A CAR SHUTTLE OPTION

If you'd prefer a shorter hike and don't mind establishing a car shuttle, you can make this a 3.2-mile, one-way walk. Park a car at the Cole Mountain Road gate. Drive your other car north on OR-53 and turn right onto Hamlet Road after approximately 6.5 miles. Before the town of Hamlet, turn right onto Hill Road, which turns into Fall Creek Road. Follow this good dirt road (suitable for passenger cars and RVs) for approximately 5 miles until you turn right onto North Fork Road. After another mile, you'll reach a gate that marks the state forest boundary. Park in a pullout along the road, walk around the gate and across the bridge over the North Fork Nehalem River. Then make the 3.2-mile hike to your car.

Salmonberry-
Nehalem Drainage

GOD'S VALLEY

45

Suggested
Maps
Mapcarta's
"Cole
Mountain"
map

With an elevation of only 371 feet above sea level, God's Valley affords hikers the opportunity to carve their own trail along the elk paths to the south of Cole Mountain.

Difficulty	Trailhead Coordinates
Easy	45.7925, -123.7345
Distance	Elevation
No set distance	100 feet gain

GETTING THERE

From Portland, drive west on US-26 to Necanicum Junction. Turn left (south) onto OR-53 and continue past milepost 13 to God's Valley Road, which is on your left. Follow God's Valley Road for 7 miles; milepost markers will serve as indicators that you are on the main road. Park anywhere in the valley after milepost 7.

There are no developed trails in the valley, which was once a homestead and is now owned by the state. You can make your own hiking route by finding and following one of many elk trails along the edges of the meadows or simply by walking through the meadow or along its creeks. Locals say there are miles of these trails. It is impossible to get lost as long as you keep to the meadows and don't wander off into the surrounding woods. If you do, however, choose to venture into the woods, do so at your own risk and make sure to pay attention to your surroundings so you can find your way back to the meadow.

If you're lucky, you might see an elk herd, coyotes, or other wildlife. Meandering creeks and wetlands make God's Valley a great place for bird watching. In early spring, the marshy areas will greet you with a profusion of bright yellow skunk cabbage. Also watch for some fairly large spruce trees. And you might come upon some apple trees from the old homestead. In the summer, there will be hundreds of blackberry bushes, both the invasive Himalayan and the native trailing blackberry. If you decide to pick some, please note that you need to be careful of the thorns. The Oregon Department of Fish and Wildlife also released turkeys in the valley, but most of them have moved to the fields along OR-53 before you turn onto God's Valley Road.

Be sure to wear pants and long sleeves; the grass in the valley is high and can scratch and irritate bare skin. Some routes also may be muddy or flooded in the rainy season. Regardless, this quiet valley is a wonderful place to explore, picnic, and meditate. You can spend just an hour or easily all day if you wish.

TRIPLE C TRAIL

An easy, well-signed, and well-maintained loop trail from Reehers Camp Day Use Area. It is designed for horses but is great for campers at Reehers Campground or for hikers looking for an easy hike in the upper Nehalem River area.

Difficulty	Trailhead Coordinates
Easy	45.70696, -123.33793

Distance	Elevation
2-mile loop	Approximately 280 feet gain

Suggested
Maps
Oregon
Hikers' Yes
Triple C Map
(not exact)

GETTING THERE
From Portland, drive west on US-26. Turn left (south) at Timber Road, between mileposts 38 and 37. Drive 3 miles to the community of Timber. Just after crossing the bridge, but before the railroad tracks, turn right on Cochran Road. It's partially paved and partially gravel but easily accessible for passenger cars. At about 2 miles, you'll see Reehers Campground on the left. Just after that, turn left into the Reehers Camp Trailhead Area.

Park at the trailhead parking area. The marked trailhead is just across Cochran

46

Photo courtesy of Brian Pasko

Road from there. Climb carefully through mixed woodland and meadows. There's a small clearcut area on the left and an old sign that says "Timber Sale Boundary" on the right. There are some big, old stumps, but this part of the trail is mostly young second growth.

Cross Wheeler Road at 1 mile, and at 1.7 miles you'll come to Cochran Road. If you turn right here you will cross a bridge over the creek and join the Gales Creek Trail, but to complete the loop, cross the road and follow the trail along the creek back to the trailhead. This is a beautiful area with lots of big old stumps and fallen trees. Imagine what it would have been like before it was logged!

In late spring the trail is colorful with a profusion of flowers, and you can hear the nuthatches, juncos, and chickadees in the trees. You can also occasionally hear very loud kingfishers in the creek.

Illustration courtesy of Lori LaBissoniere

CLATSOP STATE FOREST

SPRUCE RUN CREEK TRAIL

Departing from the Henry Rierson Spruce Run Campground, the Spruce Run Creek trail meanders to a hidden lake, akin to a large pond, that sometimes dries out in the summer. Keep an eye out for wildflowers among the thick foliage.

Difficulty
Moderate

Distance
5.6 miles

Trailhead Coordinates
45.812467, -123.61065

Elevation
1,580 feet gain

Suggested Maps
ODF Clatsop State Forest Recreation Guide

GETTING THERE

From Portland, take US-26 west toward the coast for about 53 miles. Turn left on Lower Nehalem Road following signs for Spruce Run Campground. Stay on Lower Nehalem Road for 5.5 miles and you will enter the campground. The trailhead is on the left with a pullout big enough for a few cars.

This is a pleasant hike on a well-maintained trail, but there are some very steep sections. The trail follows Spruce Run Creek the entire way, but most of the time, you will be far above it. Start your hike at the trailhead and gradually climb above the campground. As you pass the last of the

47

Photo courtesy of Brian Pasko

campsites, you will get your first view of Spruce Run Creek, which goes through the campground and then enters the Nehalem River.

In just under 0.5 miles, you will reach the first and only easy access point to a scenic spot on Spruce Run Creek. Just after this, the trail starts a steeper climb that doesn't last long and soon descends back to creek level. Over the next 0.5 miles, the trail moves slightly away from the creek and has a series of gentle slopes.

For most of the next mile, you will be going up some very steep sections of trail without much reprieve in between. To take your mind off the ascent, you can look for large stumps left over from the logging operations of long ago. When you reach about 1.8 miles, the incline finally subsides, and you can catch your breath and enjoy the forest around you.

At 2 miles, you reach a well-marked junction with a trail that leads out to a gated road that goes to Lost Lake Road. Follow this road to Spruce Run Lake. Not long after this, you will make a somewhat steep descent that will reward you with your final climb before the lake. At 2.8 miles, you reach the small but pretty Spruce Run Lake. The trail continues for a short distance along the north side of the lake but soon peters out, and the lake gets very marshy at this point as well. Return the way you came to get back to the trailhead.

Clatsop
State Forest

GNAT CREEK TRAIL

Suggested
Maps
ODF Clatsop
State Forest
Recreation
Guide;
Clatsop State
Forest Trail
Guide Astoria
District—
Highway 30:
Gnat Creek
Campground
and Trails

Gnat Creek Trail has something for every hiking enthusiast: a rich Sitka spruce forest, a view of Little Barrier Falls, glimpses of running coho salmon, and a fish hatchery along the creekside. The hike can be sectioned into three legs: first, the path to Gnat Creek Campground; second, the nature trail loop at the falls; and finally, the Upper Gnat Creek Trail.

Difficulty
Moderate

Distance
Distance 4 miles round-
trip from hatchery,
or 7 miles round-trip
from Gnat Creek
Campground

Trailhead Coordinates
46.17715, -123.504958

Elevation
Approximately 400
feet gain

GETTING THERE
From Portland, head west on US-30 (Lincoln Highway) for about 75 miles. To reach the trailhead for the Upper Gnat Creek Trail, pull into the Gnat Creek Hatchery. The hatchery is also 18 miles east of Astoria on US-30. Plenty of parking is available.

This hike is 4 miles round-trip, but if you choose to begin at the Gnat Creek Campground, the hike adds another 1.5 miles from the campground to the fish hatchery. You will hike through old stands of hemlock and spruce trees and cross US-30 (Lincoln Highway) into the Gnat Creek Fish Hatchery.

The trailhead at the hatchery begins at 200 feet, parallels the creek, and climbs to approximately 600 feet. After you cross a railed footbridge, you will see plenty of sword fern, deer fern, salal, foxglove, skunk cabbage, huckleberry and salmonberry bushes, and cascara buckthorn.

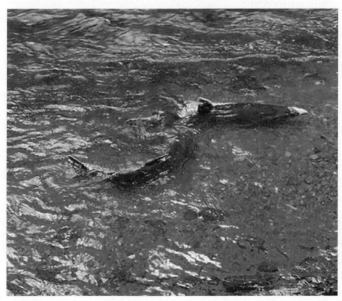

Photo courtesy of Chris Smith

Clatsop
State Forest

After a quarter mile in, you will be hiking through second-growth Douglas-firs with a smattering of western hemlock. Occasionally, you'll come across large, old-growth Sitka spruce and Douglas-fir. Unfortunately, after hiking over a mile, you will come across timber sale boundary signs that mark the hilly portion on the south side of the trail. The creek is always to your left (north), and there are a few places where you can get off the main trail and hike to Gnat Creek, which is overshadowed by big-leaf maple and red alder.

At about 2.5 miles, the trail makes a "lollipop" sort of loop before heading back down. The little loop has a bench, and there's a great view of Gnat Creek.

BLOOM LAKE

An easy route along a closed road to a small lake. The walk from the highway to Bloom Lake is good for families or as a quiet stop between Portland and the coast.

Difficulty
Easy

Distance
3.6 miles
round-trip

Trailhead Coordinates
45.838, -123.5136

Elevation
470 feet gain

Suggested
Maps
ODF 1998
Oregon
Protection
District map

Photo courtesy of Chris Smith

49

GETTING THERE

From Portland, take US-26 west toward the coast for about 50 miles until you reach mile marker 27. Park at the parking lot located right off the highway.

Beginning from the parking lot, this well-maintained, easy trail meanders through a young alder and hemlock forest. Big, blackened stumps, carbonized in the 1933 Wolf Creek fire, loom amongst the green, while birdsong fills the woods. After 20 minutes, the trail takes a right turn (at the sign) and soon arrives at Bloom Lake, a tranquil stretch of water encircled by the forest and fed by a small creek. A marshy trail to the right leads across a fallen old-growth tree and eventually to a large, old Sitka spruce. This spot offers a clearing for picnics and a nice view of the lake, which can be accessed by obscured paths.

NORTHRUP CREEK EQUESTRIAN LOOP TRAIL

Horseback riders and hikers will enjoy this trail as it meanders through beautiful coastal rainforest, passing several magnificent old-growth denizens of the Clatsop State Forest along the way. Bring water shoes for an unbridged stream crossing.

Difficulty	Trailhead Coordinates
Moderate	46.019313, -123.453266
Distance	Elevation
8.5-mile loop	1,500 feet gain

GETTING THERE

From Portland, drive west on US-26. Just past milepost 22, exit onto OR-103 (Fishhawk Falls Highway 103, the exit for Jewell and Mist) and proceed north for 9 miles. Turn right onto OR-202 (Nehalem Highway) toward Birkenfeld and Vernonia and drive 5.8 miles to Northrup Creek Road, just past milepost 35. Turn left and proceed 1.4 miles to the end of the pavement. It's another 4.8 miles on a good gravel road to the day use parking area where you'll find the trailhead.

Suggested Maps
ODF Clatsop State Forest Recreation Guide; Clatsop State Forest Trail Guide Astoria District—Highway 202: Northrup Creek Horse Camp & Trails

50

The trail starts at a signpost in the parking area and gently rises through a young Douglas-fir forest dotted with large rotting stumps from earlier logging. At 0.16 miles, cross Northrup Creek Road and follow the trail on the other side. A short descent follows, and soon thereafter you'll find yourself marveling at the stately remnants of a forest that once was—an immense western redcedar, a huge Sitka spruce, and several gargantuan big-leaf maples. Old-growth specimens such as these are rare in Oregon's coastal rainforest, so pause to enjoy them.

After paralleling Northrup Creek for more than a mile, the trail begins a 0.55 mile climb via a series of curves and gentle switchbacks, finally reaching a gravel road at 2.45 miles. Turn right on this road, and then turn right on another gravel road. At the next intersection turn left, walk for 0.2 miles, then veer left onto yet another gravel road. Keep to the right 100 feet later (avoiding the gravel quarry) and follow this undulating path through a forest of broadly spaced Douglas-firs until it ends 0.4 miles later. Follow the single track on the right.

The trail traverses a hillside for a short distance and then dives steeply for 0.2 miles to the bottom of the Northrup Creek canyon. At 3.75 miles, you reach an unbridged crossing of Northrup Creek where it may be necessary to get your feet wet. Time to use those water shoes if you brought them.

At 4 miles the trail crosses the campground entrance road and enters a clearcut replanted in 2003. It then ascends at a moderately steep grade and after 0.5 miles reaches a somewhat recent clearcut where views extend

Photo courtesy of Kristin Roosmalen

out across the forest to the east, south, and west. For the next 0.3 miles, you'll follow the old logging road, the only part of the route that offers expansive views.

At the far end of the clearcut, the trail (still a logging road) dives back into the forest and continues its moderate ascent. At 5.1 miles it reaches Cow Ridge Road (a gravel road), which you follow uphill for 20 feet to the single track on the right. The single track is short-lived, however, and you'll soon find yourself back on Cow Ridge Road. Go straight (downhill), following the road for 0.1 miles where you will rejoin the single track on the right next to a clearcut.

The trail soon enters a Douglas-fir and alder forest whose floor is rife with sword fern. Before long you'll find yourself walking through a park-like setting with Douglas-fir overhead and grassy swales dotted with clumps of sword fern at your feet. After crossing a bridge at 5.85 miles, the trail meanders for a mile through a pleasant forest of Douglas-fir, western redcedar, and western hemlock.

At 7.5 miles, switchback up into a recent clearcut, climbing at a moderate grade for 0.25 miles to a logging road. In the next 0.2 miles, you'll encounter several intersections. Turn right on the logging road, bear left at the next intersection, and then go right at the next one. Bear left at the next junction and, in approximately 150 feet, turn right onto the single-track trail.

The trail descends gently through the clearcut for 0.15 miles before re-entering the forest. From here it's a pleasant 0.7 miles woodsy walk to a junction where you turn right, toward the day use area, which is now just 0.2 miles away.

BIG TREE TRAIL

The Big Tree Trail, a loop of approximately 1 mile, begins at the group picnic site and follows Northrup Creek for much of its distance. Along the way, it passes several old-growth behemoths from the days before logging changed the landscape. Big-leaf maples up to 11 feet in diameter, a western redcedar nearly 8 feet in diameter, a Sitka spruce approaching 7 feet in diameter, and grand firs almost 6 feet in diameter are the stars of the very pleasant and worth-while walk.

PLANT LIST

* indicates poisonous plant

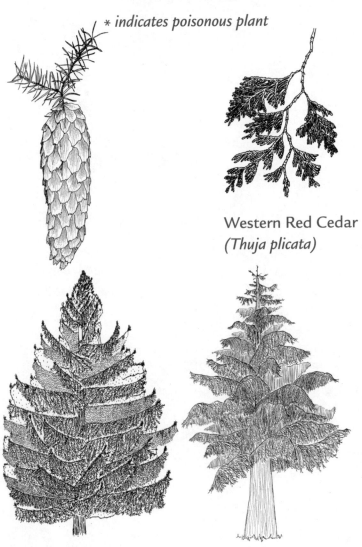

Western Red Cedar
(Thuja plicata)

Sitka Spruce
(Picea sitchensis)

Pacific Dogwood
(Cornus nuttallii)

Oregon White Oak
(Quercus garryana)

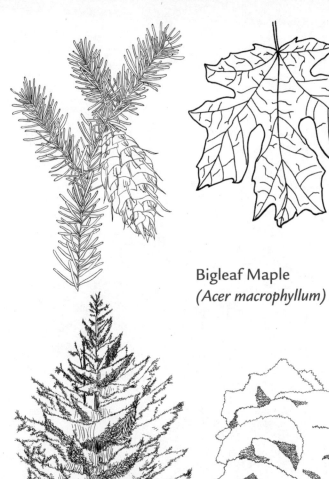

Bigleaf Maple
(Acer macrophyllum)

Douglas Fir
(Pseudotsuga menziesii)

Trillium
(Trillium ovatum)

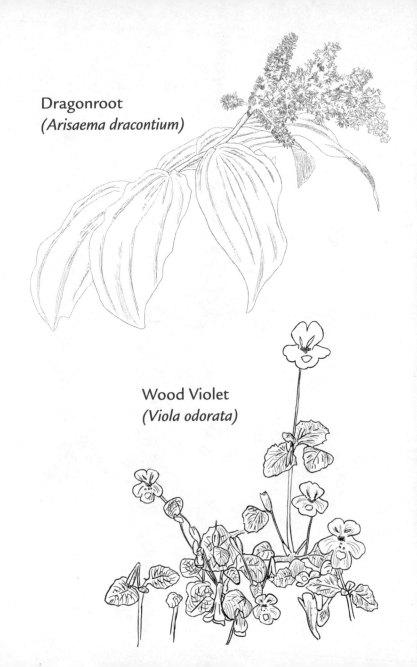

Dragonroot
(Arisaema dracontium)

Wood Violet
(Viola odorata)

Foxglove*
(Digitalis purpurea)

Fairy Slipper
(Calypso bulbosa)

212

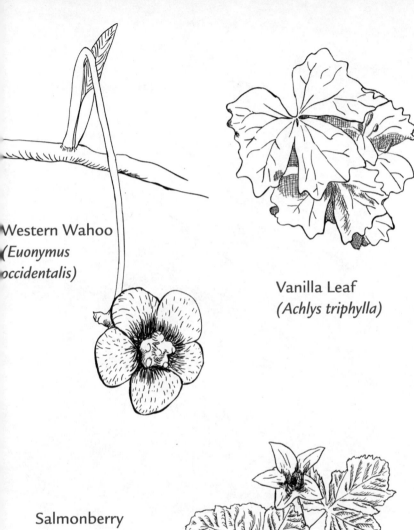

Western Wahoo
(Euonymus occidentalis)

Vanilla Leaf
(Achlys triphylla)

Salmonberry
(Rubus spectabilis)

Goat's Beard
(Aruncus dioicus)

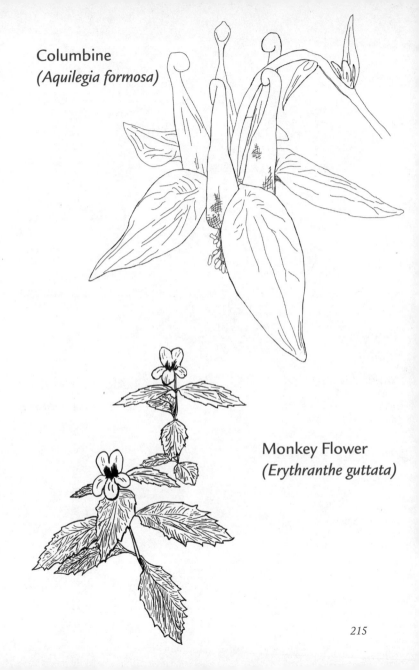

Columbine
(Aquilegia formosa)

Monkey Flower
(Erythranthe guttata)

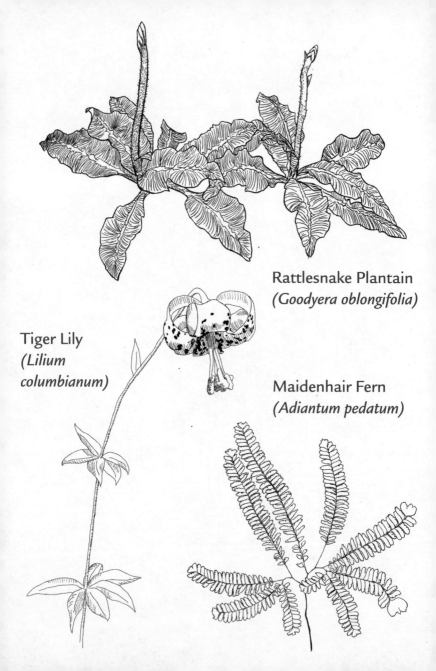

Rattlesnake Plantain
(Goodyera oblongifolia)

Tiger Lily
*(Lilium
columbianum)*

Maidenhair Fern
(Adiantum pedatum)

OTHER RESOURCES

The following reports and books may be useful if you would like to learn more about the Tillamook State Forest.

History

Epitaph of the Giants: The History of the Tillamook Burn by J. Larry Kemp. Touchstone Press. Beaverton, Oregon. 1967.

Nehalem Tillamook Tales by Clara Pearson. Oregon State University Press. Corvallis, Oregon. 1990.

Diaries of Orwin Vaughn. Warren Vaughn—his personal journals at the Oregon Historical Society Archives.

The Adventures of Dr. Huckleberry: Tillamook County, Oregon by E.R. Huckleberry. Oregon Historical Society. Portland, Oregon. 1970.

Tillamook Indians of the Oregon Coast by Bruce Johnson and John Sauter. Binford & Mort Publishing. Hillsboro, Oregon. 1974.

Tillamook Burn Country, A Pictorial History by Ellis Lucia. Caxton Printers Ltd. Caldwell, Idaho. 1983.

The Big Woods: Logging and Lumbering, from Bull Teams to Helicopters, in the Pacific Northwest by Ellis Lucia. Doubleday. Garden City, New York. 1975.

Columbia's River: The Voyages of Robert Gray, 1787–1793 by J. Richard Nokes. Washington State Historical Society. Tacoma, Washington. 1991.

The Hidden Northwest by Robert Cantwell. Lippincott. Philadelphia, Pennsylvania. 1972.

Ancient Forests and Western Man: A Pictorial History of the West Coast by Ann Amato. Frank Amato Publications. Portland, Oregon. 1992.

Pioneers of the Wilson River Stage Road by Helen Reeher Luebke. Forest Grove, Oregon.

Tillamook State Forest Policy

Northwest Oregon State Forests Management Plan by the Oregon Department of Forestry. Oregon Department of Forestry. Salem, Oregon. 2010.

Western Oregon State Forests Habitat Conservation Plan by the Oregon Department of Forestry. Oregon Department of Forestry. Salem, Oregon.

An Independent Scientific Review of ODF's Proposed Western Oregon State Forests Habitat Conservation Plan by the Oregon Department of Forestry. Oregon Department of Forestry. Salem, Oregon.

Ecosystem Recovery Alternative for State Forests by the National Wildlife Federation. National Wildlife Federation. Seattle, Washington.

Simplified Forest Management to Achieve Watershed and Forest Health: A Critique by Jerry Franklin, Christopher Frissell, David Montgomery, Reed Noss, and David Perry. National Wildlife Federation. Seattle, Washington.

Tillamook State Forest: Recreation Action Plan 2000 by the Oregon Department of Forestry. Oregon Department of Forestry. Salem, Oregon. 2000.

The Tillamook: A Created Forest Comes of Age by Gail Wells. Oregon State University Press. Corvallis, Oregon. 1999.

Fish, Plants, and Wildlife

Plants of the Pacific Northwest Coast by Andy MacKinnon and Jim Pojar. Lone Pine Publishing. Auburn, Washington. 1994.

Plants and Animals of the Pacific Northwest: An Illustrated Guide to the Natural History of Western Oregon, Washington and British Columbia by Eugene Kozloff. University of Washington Press. Seattle, Washington. 1976.

National Audubon Society Field Guide to the Pacific Northwest by Peter Alden and Dennis Paulson. Alfred A. Knopf, Inc. New York City, New York. 1998.

Rare and Endangered Plants of Oregon by Donald C. Eastman. Beautiful America Publishing. Woodburn, Oregon. 1990.

Mushrooms Demystified by David Arora. Ten Speed Press. Berkeley, California. 1979.

Fishing in Oregon: The Complete Oregon Fishing Guide by Madelynne Diness. Flying Pencil Publishing. Oregon. 1984.

An Angler's Astoria by Dave Hughes. Frank Amato Publications. Milwaukie, Oregon. 1982.

Tracking and the Art of Seeing How to Read Animal Tracks and Signs by Paul Rezendes. Camden House Publishing. Columbia, South Carolina. 1992.

A Manual of the Higher Plants of Oregon by Morton Eaton Peck. Binford & Mort Publishing. Hillsboro, Oregon. 1961.

INDEX

OOLIGAN PRESS

Ooligan Press is a student-run publishing house rooted in the rich literary culture of the Pacific Northwest. Founded in 2001 as part of Portland State University's Department of English, Ooligan is dedicated to the art and craft of publishing. Students pursuing master's degrees in book publishing staff the press in an apprenticeship program under the guidance of a core faculty of publishing professionals.

PROJECT MANAGERS
Sophie Aschwanden
T. J. Carter

PROJECT TEAM
James Bezerra
Eric Bronson
Bridget Carrick
Jessica DeBolt
Sarah Eggleston
Lisa Hein
Stephen Hyde
Kento Ikeda
Ben Kessler
Sadie Moses
Morgan Nicholson
Liz Pilcher

Riley Pittenger
Nada Sewidan
Thomas Spoelhof
Pam Wells
Desiree Wilson

ACQUISITIONS
Vi La Bianca
Maeko Bradshaw
Stephanie Argy
Terence Brierly
T. J. Carter
Mackenzie Deater
Taylor Farris
Hope Levy
Amylia Ryan

EDITING
Lisa Hein
Hilary Louth
Eric Bronson
T. J. Carter
Bridget Carrick
Mackenzie Deater
Jessica DeBolt
Grace Evans
Katie Fairchild
Michele Ford
Emily HagenBurger
Elizabeth Hughes
Kento Ikeda
Hope Levy
Rachel Lulich
Scott MacDonald
Sadie Moses
Amylia Ryan
Alyssa Schaffer
Thomas Spoelhof
Joanna Szabo
Pam Wells

DESIGN
Andrea McDonald
Bridget Carrick

Hope Levy
Riley Pittenger
Pam Wells

DIGITAL
Stephanie Argy
Kento Ikeda

MARKETING
Jordana Beh
Morgan Nicholson
Jessica DeBolt
Stephen Hyde
Kento Ikeda
Ben Kessler
Nada Sewidan
Desiree Wilson

SOCIAL MEDIA
Katie Fairchild
Terence Brierly
Bridget Carrick
Elise Hitchings
Stephen Hyde
Sadie Moses
Liz Pilcher
Riley Pittenger

COLOPHON

This book is set in ITC Legacy Serif and Sans Serif, two fonts designed to be complementary to each other through sharing the same skeletal structure. Created in 1992 by Ronald Arnholm, ITC Legacy was inspired by the roman type of Nicholas Jenson from 1470, which Arnholm encountered while attending graduate school at Yale University. After years of work, Arnholm succeeded in creating a font family with serifs and sans serifs, italics, and a complete set of weights to choose from.